THE 21-DAY REVIVAL

A WHOLE FOOD AND NUTRITION PROGRAM
FOR A HEALTHY BODY

Dr. Joshua Levitt

UpWellness
Nutrient-Rich Living

CONTENTS

Taming The Fire of Chronic Inflammation

There is nothing quite like the sickening feeling you get when your toe smashes into the corner of the coffee table. We've all been there and experienced that pain and the redness, heat, and swelling that goes along with it. No matter what caused it, if it's red, hot, painful, and swollen...it's inflamed.

Inflammation is a protective immune response to a harmful or dangerous stimulus. It is normal, natural, and an essential part of the healing process. The word inflammation is derived from the Latin root word inflammare which means to ignite or set ablaze.

Paleolithic humans figured out how to control and harness the power of fire and we have depended on it for cooking and warmth ever since. On the flip side, of course, uncontrolled fire is one of the most destructive forces on the planet. Fire truly is a blessing and a curse. And so is inflammation... just like the fire from which it derives its name.

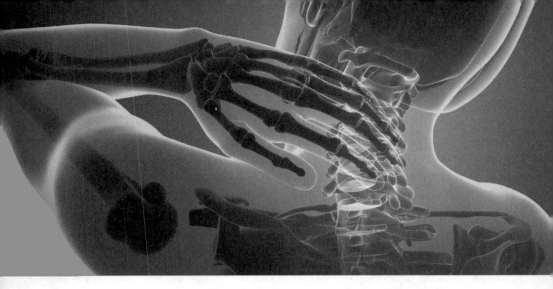

Inflammation is an absolutely essential biological reaction that we cannot survive without. But when that essential process gets out of control, it can become a destructive force—one that is at the root of virtually all painful and chronic diseases.

Taming the fire of chronic inflammation is entirely within your control. The switches on the inflammation control panel can be controlled by your own dietary and lifestyle choices. Poor choices act like wind on a forest fire and they cause inflammation to flare up which increases the risk of illness and pain. Good choices are like the rain; they cool down the inflammation and decrease the risk of chronic disease.

This 21-day program is going to give you the tools that you need to be the captain of the fire department that will get the flames of inflammation under control. You'll learn everything that you need to know to help you make the right choices, and you'll absolutely love the results. You can expect to lose weight (if you need to), and see improvements in your energy level, your mood, your skin, and your digestion. As an added bonus, there will also be a host of improvements that you cannot easily see on the outside but you'll see on your next blood tests. People who follow the advice in this program will see across the board improvements in blood sugar, cholesterol, and laboratory markers of inflammation that correspond to decreased risk of chronic disease. The program materials come in three main parts:

The 21-Day Revival Food and Nutrition Guide

This is the section of the book that you are reading right now. You can think of this as Part One. In it, you'll learn all about inflammation and why getting it under control should be your primary health goal. Part One also provides you with an overview of how The 21-Day Revival program is designed... you'll find that on the next few pages. After the overview, we'll have a detailed discussion of the three major macronutrient groups: protein, fat, and carbohydrates and how the foods within each group fit into the program. Part One finishes up with information about micronutrients (like vitamins and minerals), herbal medicines, and the most important lifestyle considerations for decreasing inflammation.

The 21-Day Revival Program Manual

This section serves as the guide for the entire 21-Day Revival program. You'll use this manual as your day-by-day guide as you move through the program. It contains the lists of "foods to include" and "foods to avoid" for each phase of the program which you'll be looking at every day. This manual also includes a daily lesson for each of the 21 days of the program which will enhance the effects of the diet and lifestyle changes you'll be making.

Program Overview

The following is a brief overview of The 21-Day Revival program. This will give you a sense of the overall architecture and design of the experience. This section is a summary; you'll get more detailed food lists and guidance in the next section.

The program is divided into three sections, which are outlined below

Phase One:
Days 1-7 (Usually Saturday-Friday)

This first phase takes care of some important internal housekeeping. I like to call it the "basic clean up." In this portion of the program, you will be eating a clean diet that includes lots of familiar foods so you will not feel hungry or deprived. Your diet will be densely packed with nutrients and you'll be putting the focus on eliminating the common triggers of inflammation and increasing the overall nutrient density of your diet.

You will phase out "junk" foods and drinks, especially those that contain high fructose corn syrup. You will eliminate white carbohydrates and replace them with whole grain sources. You will learn why it is critical that you cut out factory-farmed animal products but you'll be free to eat "clean" meat, poultry, fish, eggs, and dairy products. You will be avoiding processed foods with their long lists of ingredients and will be building meals based on a list of whole, single-ingredient foods.

In addition to the changes that you'll make to your diet, you will also be making some simple lifestyle modifications as well. We are going to limit alcohol and caffeine to one drink per day. Cooking and preparing your own meals becomes a bigger part of your life. You will be doing gentle physical activity each day as well as developing daily habits that will bring natural health and wellness into your lifestyle.

Phase Two:
Days 8-14 (Usually Saturday-Friday)

We are going to kick it up a notch this week! During this period, you will be hitting your stride and developing the dietary and lifestyle habits that are part of your long-term solution. You'll begin to add in more plant-based superfoods and decrease your animal protein significantly. You'll decrease your sugar intake even further and you'll cut back alcohol to two drinks per week. A greater percentage of your food should be coming from your own kitchen.

Phase Two is really important to get comfortable with because it is the portion of this program that most closely resembles the eating pattern that you should strive to continue when this program is over. It is not a vegetarian diet but it is power-packed with plant-based foods which are associated with decreased inflammation and reduced risk of chronic disease. This is the way that the longest-lived people in the world tend to eat, so it is clearly a long-term, sustainable solution.

Phase Three:
Days 15-21 (Usually Saturday-Friday)

At this point in the program, your body and mind are ready to explore some uncharted territory. Your diet will be pristine! This week is seven days of optimized human nutrition, maximal anti-inflammatory eating, no compromise. Phase Three is intense and designed to be a challenge.

Phase Three begins with a big weekend event: a 48-hour liquid only fast! For two days, you will be consuming an abundance of easily digestible nutrients in the form of blended drinks, smoothies, juices, soups, broths, and teas. Liquid nutrition for 48 hours is a safe and effective way to jumpstart your anti-inflammatory biochemistry without compromising your nutrition. Your immune system uses vitamins, minerals, and phytonutrients for fuel so optimizing the absorption of these compounds is an excellent way to enhance the anti-inflammatory process.

This 48-hour period is when you really turn the corner on the road to a revitalized diet and lifestyle. During these two days, it is generally best to keep your schedule as empty as possible. You will be putting extra energy into the lessons on lifestyle change and stress management and you'll want to minimize distractions in order to maintain your focus. This weekend is a turning point for you...the road ahead is coming into view.

In the remainder of Phase Three, you'll be eating a plant-based diet, primarily vegetarian with a little twist (small amounts of premium animal protein will be allowed). You will be eliminating wheat, gluten, and most dairy products as well. It will be a big change from the way you used to eat. During this period, you will get acquainted with some new foods and flavors, and begin to notice what it feels like to be optimally nourished.

Along with the improvements that you'll feel in your body, like increased energy, better sleep, improved mood, and better digestion, you'll also begin to assimilate the dietary and lifestyle improvement that you've been learning into a daily routine that will ultimately become a longer-term, sustainable plan for the future.

Food Rules:
During all phases of this program there are a few basic food rules:

- Eat only during a 12-hour period each day. (For example, if you eat breakfast at 7am, you should be done with dinner by 7pm...and not eat again until breakfast the next day.)

- Eat meals and snacks slowly while sitting down.

- Your first and second meals of the day must include a portion of clean protein.

- Dinner should include a protein source but not required.

- Meals must contain a vegetable.

- No seconds.

- Up to two healthy snacks per day if you are hungry.

- No food for at least 2 hours before bedtime.

Inflammation 101

In order to understand how the food and lifestyle choices you make can affect the inflammatory process, it really helps to have a basic scientific understanding of how the process works. Inflammation is a function of the immune system, and what follows here is a simple, non-technical overview of how the system works so that you can learn to control it on your own.

In the first year of medical school, doctors learn a few rhyming Latin words that describes all the elements of the inflammatory process: Dolor, calor, rubor, tumor, functio laesa. Please allow me to translate for you:

Dolor:
This means pain. Inflammation hurts. The pain is caused by the release of a family of chemical compounds which stimulate the nerve endings at the site.

Calor:
This means heat. The inflamed area gets hot as a result of increased blood flow and additional chemical mediators that raise temperature.

Rubor:
This means redness. Now we're red, hot, and painful. Like heat, redness is caused by increases in local blood flow.

Tumor:
This means swelling or abnormal growth. An area that is inflamed gets engorged with blood, fluid, cells, and all of the chemical messengers of the healing process. All that stuff accumulates at the site and the area puffs up swollen. It is important to note here that inflammation and swelling are not the same thing. Swelling without the heat, pain, and redness is not inflammation. A great example of this is "edema." We've all seen puffy lower legs and feet, like when socks or stockings leave deep lines on the feet or lower legs. That is edema (swelling) but not inflammation.

Functio Laesa:
This refers to loss of function. Unfortunately, it doesn't rhyme like the rest of the descriptors but loss of function is a part of the inflammatory process, and it's one that can cause great distress in any body region.

Taking A Closer Look At
The Inflammatory Process

Going back to our example about the stubbed toe at the beginning. Let's take a closer look at what is actually occurring in the toe just after it smashes into the table all the way up to the point when you see and feel the redness, heat, pain, and swelling.

The toe hitting the table causes tissue damage. As the soft tissue within the toe gets crushed, blood vessels and soft tissue cells break open and release their contents into the local area. The appearance of this material that is normally kept inside the cell or within blood vessels causes an alarm that signals to the local immune system that there is damage that needs to be repaired.

The local immune system then uses an array of molecular signals to call in for additional support from the systemic (whole body) immune system. At this point we start to see the migration of white blood cells and a whole cocktail of chemical messengers that are part of the inflammatory reaction.

For those of you who really want to impress your friends, the ingredients in that inflammatory chemical cocktail includes families of compounds called cytokines, prostaglandins, interleukins, thromboxanes, and leukotrienes as well as some individual compounds with names that sound like college fraternities like TNF-alpha and NF-kappaB. All of these compounds are individual players in the chain reaction of events that results in a full-blown immune system reaction in the damaged area.

Redness, heat, pain, swelling, and loss of function are the end result.

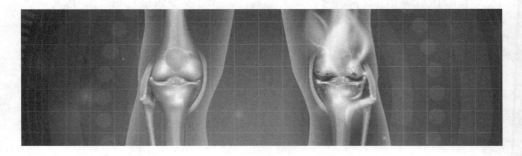

You Are What You Eat

We have all experienced an inflammatory reaction. If you want a quick example, just scratch the inside of your arm with a fingernail and wait a few seconds. As you observe the red, puffy line that appears, it easy to understand that the intensity of the response (i.e. how aggressive it is and how long it lasts) is directly related to the severity of the stimulus that triggered it. In other words, a minor injury will cause a weak reaction, and a severe injury will cause a major reaction.

With that in mind, it is important to understand that there is another factor that is entirely unrelated to the trigger that can exert a major influence on the severity and the duration of the inflammatory reaction. That factor has to do with the very composition of our cells themselves.

You have probably heard that our bodies are composed of around 60 percent water. That leaves about 40 percent of other stuff...which is mostly flesh and bone. All of that "other stuff" is made entirely out of what you eat. When your cells are built with quality building materials, they simply work better. When cells work better, they can deal with an inflammatory stimulus more effectively.

Here is a painful story to explain how this works.

There are two adult twin brothers who are both back home and sleeping at their parent's house for a family reunion. One of them is a junk food addict, smokes cigarettes, drinks excessively, sleeps terribly, and generally doesn't take good care of himself. (Mom and dad disapprove.) The other eats healthy, whole food and is on a plant-based diet. He gets regular physical activity, plenty of sleep, and takes really good care of his health. (The golden child.) They both wake up in the middle of the night to pee. Heading toward the bathroom and...SMASH. Both of them slam their big toe into the bedpost. They each let out a yelp and clutch the toe in pain... and the inflammatory process begins.

Both toes hurt. Both toes swell up. But there is a difference that becomes clear in the next few days. One toe heals quickly, the swelling goes down and the pain resolves within three days. The other remains painful and swollen for weeks. I don't think I need to tell you who's still limping...

I hope that story helps you understand that your dietary and lifestyle choices put you in direct control of your own inflammatory response.

Poor choices ➞ More Inflammation

Good choices ➞ Less Inflammation

To understand the definition of a "good choice," we will now take a deeper dive into the nutritional building blocks of your immune system and the entire body that it defends.

Macronutrients: The Building Blocks of Healthy Cells

Gaining control over inflammation starts with better composition of your cells themselves—and even more importantly, the membranes that surround them.

Every one of the 37 trillion cells in our body is encased by an outer cell membrane which contains the contents of the cell and acts like a gatekeeper for substances to flow into or out of the cell. This flow of molecular messages across the cell membrane is the way that cells can communicate with each other. The cell membrane is essential for cellular communication because all of those chemical messages get transmitted and received across the cell membrane.

Inflammation is a process that relies on cell-to-cell communication, which is why the health and the composition of the cell membrane is of critical importance to the process.

The quality of the materials used in construction matters—a lot. (This applies to virtually any building material. For example, as a mediocre guitar player, I can assure you that even I sound better when I play a high-end instrument constructed of the finest hardwoods.) When cell membranes are constructed with "healthy" building materials, cellular communication is improved and the process of inflammation will be less severe even when the triggering stimulus is identical... just like in our twin brothers story with the stubbed toes.

So what are cell membranes made of? This may surprise you: they are composed almost entirely of fat. That's right, fat molecules. Science-types call them "lipids." These aren't just any fats either, your cell membranes are made of the very fat that you eat. This is exactly why our discussion about the building blocks of healthy cells starts with fats and oils.

Fat And Oil

Nutrition science divides fats and oils into three main categories:

Saturated Fats

These are fats that are generally solid at room temperature. Butter, lard, animal fat, and coconut oil all contain significant concentrations of saturated fats. Higher concentrations of saturated fat within a cell membrane will make the membrane more stiff or rigid, which is not necessarily a good thing. Saturated fats from clean animal sources are allowed during Phase One of the program.

Monounsaturated Fats (MUFAs)

These are healthy fats which are very similar to saturated fats except for a chemical double bond between carbons within the long molecular chain. These fats are generally liquid at body temperature and will become solid when chilled. Food sources include avocados, nuts, seed, and olive oil. MUFAs can be included liberally throughout all phases of the program.

Polyunsaturated Fats (PUFAs)

These are the oils that have the greatest anti-inflammatory nutritional benefits. In their pure and fresh form, they are the healthiest of the oils but they are also very vulnerable to oxidation, rancidity, and chemical conversion into unhealthy, pro-inflammatory fats. There are two famous families of polyunsaturated fats that play an important role in the inflammatory process. They are known as "essential fatty acids" because we cannot make them...they must be consumed in the diet. The essential fatty acids are:

Omega-3 Fatty Acids These are the healthiest oils of all. The best food source is cold-water fish. Plant sources like hemp seed, flax, chia, and walnuts are great but need to be activated before they have their anti-inflammatory effects. Having cell membranes made of omega-3 oils will make you less prone to inflammation. Dietary sources of omega-3 fats are highly encouraged throughout all phases of this program.

Omega-6 Fatty Acids When omega-6 oils occupy a large percentage of your cell membranes, you will be more prone to inflammation. These less healthy fats are found in large amounts in corn oil, vegetable oil, and soybean oil. These omega-6 oils can also be chemically "hydrogenated" which turns them into "trans fats." Trans fats are used extensively in processed, packaged foods but they are devastating to cell membrane health and major promoters of inflammation. During this program, you will avoid any foods that contain "hydrogenated" or "partially hydrogenated" oils.

When it comes to inflammation, the quality of the fats that make up the cell membrane around the outside of the cell are extremely important. But the materials on the inside matter too. Internal cellular components are made of amino acids, proteins, vitamins, and minerals and, again, the quality of the building material is essential.

Protein

Dietary proteins are essential elements of human nutrition. Proteins are large, complex molecular chains that act as a major structural component of every cell in your body. The individual links in these long protein chains are called amino acids, which are truly the building blocks of life.

Some of these amino acids can be produced naturally by our bodies, others must be consumed in the diet. These critical amino acids that we are not able to manufacture on our own are called "essential amino acids" for good reason—because eating protein sources that contain those amino acids is absolutely essential.

When you consume high quality dietary protein, your body uses the acid in your stomach and special enzymes called proteases to break the protein chains apart into individual amino acids. Those amino acids are then absorbed into your bloodstream and used to build virtually all of the structural components and cellular machinery inside your body. Getting adequate amounts of these amino acids in the diet is critical for cellular functioning.

You should eat clean protein at most meals. In this program, your protein can come from animal or plant sources, although plant sources are greatly preferred. "Clean" refers to the health of the animal or plant that it came from. You're probably asking "How am I supposed to know if my steak came from a healthy cow, if my egg came from a well-fed chicken, or if my beans grew on a vigorous vine?" Below, you'll find useful information about each of the common dietary protein sources and how they fit into your diet during this program and for the rest of your life.

Plant-Based Proteins

Soy

Although the soybean is a legume just like other beans, it is discussed separately here because it is so unique and so misunderstood. Compared to other beans, soybeans have an extraordinarily high protein content. They are also full of a naturally occurring compound called isoflavones which give them some important hormonal health activity. Their high protein content has made soybeans both a staple food and a globally important commodity crop for centuries. The isoflavones and their hormonal activity has made soybeans the subject of decades of intense research and controversy about whether they are healthy or not.

Here's the answer: not all soybeans (or products made from them) are created equal. When non-genetically modified (non-GMO) soybeans are grown in organic conditions and are consumed in traditional forms like tofu, tempeh, and miso, they are perfectly healthy. Eating these foods up to three times per week is safe and healthy for everyone.

There is a dark side of the soybean story and it starts in enormous farms that grow genetically modified beans on a large scale for industrial food production. The protein and the oil within those beans are extracted and used on a massive scale in livestock feed and in a wide variety of processed foods.

If you choose to eat soy, you should only ever eat organic, non-GMO soybeans and the focus should be on soy products like edamame, tofu, miso, and tempeh rather than the modern meat and dairy substitutes made from highly processed soybeans. Over 90 percent of the soybeans in our food supply come from genetically modified crops, so you must be very cautious and attentive about reading labels on soy products to make sure that they are from organic, non-GMO sources.

Beans (Legumes)

We're going to cut straight to the bottom line here: eat more beans. Lentils, pintos, white, black, kidney, mung, garbanzo—all of them are an excellent source of clean protein, fiber, vitamins, minerals, and antioxidants. Organic beans are ideal, and I encourage you to explore beyond the familiar varieties.

There are hundreds of different types of beans; they come in a wide variety of colors, sizes, tastes, and textures. You won't find the unusual beans in cans though; they usually come dry, which means you'll need to soak them overnight and then cook them.

Although many local supermarkets and health food stores now carry a wider array of more exotic beans, you can't beat the quality and variety of my two favorite online sources for legumes:

For beans, go to Rancho Gordo (www.ranchogordo.com)

For lentils, check out Timeless Natural Food (www.timelessfood.com)

They are all delicious! Plus, some of them are so beautiful, we keep them in glass jars on a shelf so we can admire them before we cook them.

We can't leave our discussion about beans without a quick reminder of that famous rhyme, "beans, beans the musical fruit...the more you eat, the more you toot." It's true to an extent, and many people are concerned about adding beans to their diet because of a fear of developing gas and bloating.

Here's the story: Beans contain some carbohydrate molecules that humans cannot digest. When these carbs reach the lower intestine, the ecosystem of bacteria and other organisms that live there will digest them for you. If you have a healthy, balanced ecosystem, you can eat as many beans as you want and not notice a thing. If your ecosystem is unhealthy, eating beans will prove that to you by giving you gas.

Don't worry though, for most people this problem is very easy to overcome. Here are the top six tips on avoiding gas from eating beans:

1. **Eat more beans.** Seriously. Start small and gradually increase the amount you eat and your body will "learn" to produce more of the enzymes necessary for digestion.

2. **The squish test.** Make sure that the beans you are eating are soft. You should be able to easily squish the bean between your tongue and the roof of your mouth. If you can't do the "squish test," your bean may be undercooked.

3. **Soak and rinse:** If you have dry beans and soak them overnight, discard the water you soaked them in and cook them in new, fresh water. (Use the discarded soaking water on your houseplants or garden.)

4. **Kombu:** If you cook your own beans, adding a small piece of the seaweed "Kombu" to the cooking liquid can help to reduce the gas. You can find kombu at a health food store.

5. **Digestive enzymes:** A nutritional supplement that contains digestive enzymes can be a huge help to people who get gassy or bloated from beans or other foods.

6. **Probiotics:** Eating fermented foods or taking a probiotic supplement can help to restore the balance of the organisms that live in the GI tract which can reduce gas production.

Nuts And Seeds

Nuts and seeds are fantastic food. They are among the most health-promoting foods you can eat and you should aim to eat them every day. Nuts and seeds are natural nutrition powerhouses that provide an excellent source of plant-based protein, healthy omega-3 oils, and loads of vitamins and minerals. People who eat nuts every day have been shown to live longer and have lower risks of chronic disease.

Because they are so easy to carry, have an excellent shelf life, and require no preparation or refrigeration, it's hard to imagine a better snack food. Nut butters can be added to smoothies or can be a great snack combined with fruit or vegetables. It's easy to learn to make your own nut milks which are a tasty and a healthy alternative to cow's milk. Unless you are allergic, you should aim to eat one to two handfuls of raw or lightly roasted nuts every day.

Animal Protein

Animal protein is one of the most controversial issues in all of human nutrition. Humans are omnivores, which means that we can survive on foods derived from animals, plants, or both. In terms of maximizing human health and longevity, it is clear from mountains of research that plant-based diets are ideal.

"Plant-based" does not mean only plants. It simply means that the majority of the food we eat should be from plants. Meat, fish and fowl can be a part of healthy diet, but these foods (especially the four-legged and the birds) are grossly over eaten by most Americans. Michael Pollan described the ideal diet brilliantly in just a few words when he said:

"Eat food, not too much, mostly plants." Now, on to our discussion of animal protein.

Fish

Because of its excellent amino acid profile and high levels of healthy omega-3 oils, fish is unquestionably the healthiest source of animal protein. Unfortunately, finding a clean source is not always so easy.

Wild or farm-raised, the flesh of a fish will contain the toxins and pollutants from the water in which it swims in and the food that it eats. My favorite choices for the cleanest and most eco-friendly fish are wild Alaskan salmon, farmed arctic char, sardines, anchovies, herring, as well as the occasional Alaskan halibut, mahi-mahi and black cod. As a general rule, swimming fish are cleaner than bottom-feeders or filter-feeding animals like lobster, catfish, crab, clams and mussels.

> *An excellent source for further information about the cleanest (and most eco-friendly) fish sources can be found at seafood.edf.org. You should aim to eat fish from the approved list at least three times per week.*

Meat

You should only ever eat meat from organic, grass-fed, wild, or pasture-raised animals. Meat from factory-farmed, grain-fed cows and pigs is toxic food. It is one of the most important foods to avoid while you are on this program and beyond.

If you choose to eat red meat, the health of the animal that it comes from should concern you. Conventional factory farms raise hormone treated animals on unnatural diets in crowded and confined spaces. These unhealthy conditions increase the risk of infectious diseases, so animals are also regularly treated with antibiotics.

There is no place for this sort of meat in your diet. The types of fats and oils that are present in wild or pasture-raised animals are substantially different and far better for you than the fats in conventionally fed animals. Organic, grass-fed, wild or pasture-raised meat is acceptable but should be kept to less than three meals per week. The specifics of how often you can eat red meat in this program are detailed in the program manual.

Poultry

Meat from a healthy chicken or turkey can be a good source of lean, high-quality protein. Unfortunately, the poultry that you'll find at most supermarkets comes from birds raised on unnatural diets, in cramped quarters, on huge farms that aren't really concerned about your health.

Meat from these farms contains residues of the chemicals in the feed as well as the hormones and antibiotics that were administered to the birds. You should only eat poultry that is free-range and USDA certified organic. Organic, free-range chicken and turkey is safe to consume up to three meals per week, generally. The specifics of how often you can eat poultry in this program are detailed in the program manual.

Eggs

Eggs can be a part of a healthy anti-inflammatory diet. They are full of high-quality protein, essential fatty acids, vitamins, minerals and carotenoids. The yolks contain some cholesterol, but there is no convincing evidence that eating eggs significantly increases your risk of heart disease. This is especially true when other sources of unclean animal protein (i.e., conventional beef and dairy) are kept to a minimum.

But there's a catch: eggs that come from large factory farms have been shown to have lower levels of beneficial nutrients as well as higher levels of toxins. Not surprisingly, the healthiest eggs come from the healthiest chickens. If you keep other sources of animal-derived protein to a minimum, you can safely enjoy about one egg per day.

Dairy

Technically, dairy refers to the milk from any mammal, although the vast majority of dairy in the modern diet comes from cows. For many people, dairy products find their way into virtually every meal. It's the milk in the morning cereal, the cream in the coffee, the butter on the bread and the cheese melted over the pasta or pizza for dinner. Considering that about 33 percent of Americans are lactose intolerant, dairy at every meal is way too much.

The healthiest choice in the dairy case is organic plain yogurt. Not vanilla... plain. The "probiotic" organisms that helped to ferment the milk and turn it into yogurt are beneficial themselves and they yield a higher protein content and easier-to-digest product than milk itself.

Generally, you should work to decrease your consumption of cow's milk dairy products and get comfortable with plant-based alternatives. A small amount of organic milk and cheese are acceptable but your main dairy source should be organic, plain yogurt.

Protein Powders

 By now you've begun to realize that the majority of the food that you should be eating is minimally processed and as close as possible to its natural form. As such, it may surprise you to see store-bought protein powders on our list of acceptable sources of clean, high-quality protein.

Fast-paced lives and challenging work schedules can make it difficult to find high-quality clean protein at every meal. Using a protein powder in a smoothie or stirred into food can help to fill that void for many people. Protein powders made from hemp, whey, rice, egg or pea can provide a tasty and easy way to meet your daily protein needs.

Carbohydrate

It is hard to believe that a molecule that contains nothing but carbon (C), hydrogen (H), and oxygen (O) could inspire so much nutritional controversy. Carbohydrates are ring-shaped molecules that are widely distributed in plant foods like vegetables, fruits and grains.

When these compounds are eaten, your digestive process will break them down into simple sugar molecules which serve as your body's primary fuel source. Depending on the arrangements of those Cs, Hs and Os, carbohydrates are called simple or complex. Simple carbs break down into sugar quickly and easily while complex carbs take more time to release their sugars into the bloodstream.

Whether it's a vegetable, fruit or grain, the more complex the better. Complex carbohydrates from veggies, fruits and grains are allowed and encouraged. You'll see on your food lists that the complex carbohydrate section is divided into three categories: vegetables, fruits and whole grains. Each category is discussed separately below.

Vegetables

When Hippocrates famously said "let thy food be thy medicine and medicine be thy food," he was undoubtedly referring to vegetables. You've heard it from your mother, from your doctor, and you've heard it from almost every nutrition or diet book ever published. And you're going to hear it again here! That's right, "eat your vegetables."

As a rich source of complex carbohydrates, fiber, vitamins, minerals and phytonutrients, vegetables are the ultimate health food. They are foundational foods during all three phases of this program. There are several common questions that arise when people are starting to add additional vegetables into their diet.

The following FAQ's will help you guide your vegetable decision-making.

Are organic vegetables better?

The short answer to this question is yes. It's true that organically grown produce tends to be more expensive and many people question whether the increased cost is justified. There is also an ongoing controversy about whether organic produce has more nutrients than those grown conventionally. I'd like to set the record straight...

Organic food is worth it for three reasons:

- It is better for you.
- Organic growing is better for farmers.
- Organic farms are better for the planet.

Fruits and vegetables grown in rich, fertile organic soil tend to have higher nutrient levels than their conventional counterparts. Perhaps more importantly, organically grown vegetables contain little to none of the toxic herbicides and pesticides found on (and in) conventionally grown varieties. More of what you want, less of what you don't. Although it is better to eat conventional vegetables than none at all, organic vegetables should be purchased whenever they are available and affordable.

The Environmental Working Group publishes an annual list of the "dirty dozen" which represents the most contaminated foods in the produce section. These are the foods that you should buy organic whenever possible. They also list a group of the "clean 15" which represents foods that don't tend to have large amounts of pesticide residue even when they are not grown organically.

To see a summary of the dirty dozen and clean 15,
visit the Shoppers Guide To Pesticides In Produce:
www.ewg.org/foodnews/summary.php

Are Frozen Or Canned Vegetables Okay?

Remember the old Popeye cartoon? He was big and strong because he ate his spinach, right? And his spinach was in a can! Overcooked, over-salted and not exactly tasty. Gross. Well, these days, canning and freezing technology has improved immensely and canned or frozen vegetables are much better in terms of both taste and nutrition than they were years ago.

Fresh vegetables are always preferred but frozen or canned vegetables are perfectly acceptable. Our supermarkets are brimming year-round with fresh vegetables, many of which have traveled thousands of miles to get there. When you are shopping for vegetables, it makes sense to pay attention to where you live, the season of the year, and how far away from you that fresh vegetable was grown. When fresh produce is unavailable or expensive because it is out of season, canned or frozen vegetables are an excellent choice.

If you do choose canned vegetables, make sure that the can is not lined with Bisphenol-A (BPA). This is especially true for acidic foods like tomatoes and tomato sauces which should only be bought in glass or BPA-free cans. Also, take the time to look at the label of any canned vegetable to make sure that it does not contain additives, preservatives or extra salt.

Does It Matter If My Produce Is Locally Grown?

It makes financial, environmental and nutritional sense to eat locally grown produce. When you choose locally grown produce, you will also be "eating with the seasons," which is a wonderful way to stay in touch with where your food comes from. Locally grown produce is always encouraged but not required.

Are Some Vegetables Better Than Others?

In terms of their overall nutritional value and the research on health promotion and disease prevention, there is one family of vegetables that stands way ahead of the rest. And the winner is: Brassica oleracea!

Huh? Never heard of it? Brassica oleracea is the Latin name for a group of similar plants known as "cruciferous vegetables" because their flowers resemble a cross. This group of all-stars includes broccoli, cabbage, kale, collard greens, Brussels sprouts, cauliflower and bok choy.

There is a staggering amount of medical research on the health benefits of cruciferous vegetables, including a large body of evidence about the role these plants play in anti-inflammation, human detoxification and cancer prevention. Anyone who is interested in generally improving their health should eat more cruciferous vegetables.

What Are Nightshades?

Nightshade is the common name used to describe the Solanaceae family of plants. This is a diverse group of edible, medicinal and sometimes poisonous plants. Nightshade plants contain a group of chemicals called alkaloids that can be a problem for some people with joint pain, muscle aches and certain neurologic problems. The most common nightshades in the diet are:

- Tomato

- Eggplant

- Potato (white and yellow; sweet potato is in a different plant family)

- Pepper (including bell pepper and hot pepper but not black pepper)

Some people with joint pain, headaches and other symptoms find that they feel better if they avoid nightshades. If you think that you might be reacting to nightshades, you'll get the opportunity to avoid them during Phase Three and see if it makes a difference in the way you feel. If you notice a big change, consider keeping them out of your diet for an additional 14 days. Then, try reintroducing them for one day and pay close attention to whether or not your symptoms return.

For the purposes of general health and nutrition, I am much more concerned that you actually eat the vegetables than I am about the way that they are prepared. If you can prepare them in a way that will make you more likely to eat them, that's the best way. In my family, we eat vegetables at every meal—either in a way that "highlights" them as a stand-alone dish or cooking them into a more involved recipe. My favored prep methods for stand-alone vegetables are:

1. **Roasted:** Spread a single layer of vegetables on a cookie sheet. Drizzle with olive oil and a little salt and pepper. Put in a 400° Fahrenheit oven and toss every ten minutes until they get browned and tender. This works for just about anything but it is especially great for Brussels sprouts, broccoli, beets, cauliflower, asparagus, onions, carrots, sweet potato, squash and any root vegetables. Add a squeeze of fresh lemon juice after cooking.

2. **Steamed:** Lightly steamed vegetables prepared with no added fats or oils are an excellent choice for broccoli, green beans, artichokes, carrots and cauliflower. Try cooking them just until the vegetables turn a deep rich color, while there is still a little crunch left. A steamer pot with a glass lid can be your friend.

3. **Sautéed:** Get your pan hot first, then add a bit of olive or coconut oil. This method works great for just about any single vegetable or vegetable medley. Toss in your onions, peppers, mushrooms, asparagus and zucchini, then let 'em sizzle. Take them off the heat well before they are limp.

4. **Grilled:** If barbecues could talk, mine would tell a very different story than most. Our family grill almost never cooks meat; fish and vegetables are what it knows best. Whether on a skewer, in a basket, or straight on the grate, grilled onions, corn, tomatoes, asparagus, peppers, mushrooms, eggplant, zucchini and squash taste excellent grilled. Make sure to lightly brush them with a little homemade marinade—delicious!

5. **Raw:** Some of the vitamins and phytochemicals that make vegetables so nutritious can be destroyed by heat. As such, it makes sense to eat some of your vegetables raw from time to time. When I'm preparing vegetables for a meal, I'll often cut off a few broccoli or cauliflower florets and just eat them raw while I'm cooking. Also, try snacking on raw carrots, cabbage, celery, peppers, radishes and cucumbers.

Fruit

There was a time not long ago when a piece of fresh fruit was a rare and very special treat. Back then, fresh fruit really was nature's candy, and nobody needed to be told to eat more of it. With all the other sugar-laden candy that is available these days, fruit doesn't get anywhere near enough attention. Fruits are loaded with a rainbow of healthy phytonutrients, vitamins and minerals. They make for sweet and delicious snacks and desserts. Fruit is healthy and is strongly encouraged throughout all three phases of this program.

There are several common questions that arise when people are thinking about adding additional fruit into the diet:

Is The Sugar In Fruit Bad For Me?

You may have heard about the "glycemic index," which is a scientifically valid scale that rates foods according to the rate that they raise your blood sugar. Foods with a higher glycemic index will raise blood sugar more rapidly than those with lower numbers.

Because of the natural sugars found in fruits, many of them are fairly high on the glycemic index scale which causes lots of confusion for people who don't know whether or not fruit should be included in the diet. Let's set the record straight here: you can—and should—eat fruit. The natural sugars in fruit consumed in reasonable quantities are not triggers for inflammation, which is why the food lists for each of the three phases of this program include fruit.

Fresh Or Frozen?

Generally speaking, fresh fruits are ideal, but there are several advantages to freezing. For many recipes, frozen fruit performs perfectly well and is significantly less expensive. Frozen fruits are perfect for making a nice thick smoothie without adding extra ice. And of course, because they have a much longer shelf life, frozen or canned foods can make summer fruits available all year long.

What About Dried Fruit?

When a fruit is dried and the water is evaporated, what's left is a concentrated version of the original. Although there is nothing unhealthy about the drying process itself, eating dried fruits does present two common problems:

The sugars in dried fruits are much more concentrated and it's easy to eat much more than you should. A good rule for dried fruits is that you should only eat as much dried fruit as you would have if that fruit were fresh. Think about those dried apricot slices. Each one (sometimes two) of those was a whole apricot. How many fresh whole apricots would you eat in one sitting?

Dried fruits often contain additives and preservatives to help maintain freshness, color, or texture. These chemical additives should be avoided entirely.

Does My Fruit Need To Be Organic?

As discussed above for vegetables, it is always better to buy organic fruit when it is available and affordable. I would prefer you to buy frozen organic fruit over conventional fresh fruit. As noted previously on Page 39, the Environmental Working Group produces an annual list of the "dirty dozen" and the "clean 15" (referring to all produce). Use it as a handy shopping guide to help you make purchasing decisions regarding the most and least contaminated fruits.

Sweeteners

It wasn't very long ago when getting your hands on a sugar cube was a rare and special treat. About 300 years ago, the average person ate about five pounds of sugar per year. Today, the average person consumes nearly 200 pounds of sugar per year! There is a very old phrase in toxicology that says "the dose makes the poison" which expresses the idea that even a harmless substance can be a toxin...it all depends on the dose. In the case of modern day sugar consumption, the dose is most definitely toxic.

In the quantities that are currently consumed by the average person, sugar is toxic—plain and simple. It causes diabetes and increases inflammation, which hastens the development of heart disease and cancer. You should decrease your sugar consumption significantly. Naturally occurring sugars like honey and maple syrup are generally acceptable, but you should be adding these in yourself rather than letting a food manufacturer add them for you.

Let's take a close look at vanilla yogurt for an example of how this can work for you. If you look at the label of a typical plain unflavored yogurt, you'll see that one cup contains about nine grams of naturally occurring milk sugar. A store bought vanilla yogurt usually contains nearly 30 grams. Quick math quiz: 30-9 = ? You got it... the manufacturer added 21 grams of sugar to the yogurt to give it that sweet vanilla flavor.

Why not just add your own? If you buy the plain yogurt and add one teaspoon of your own real maple syrup and a few drops of vanilla extract, your total sugar will be about 13 to 15 grams. Less than half of the store bought version! (Hint: sugar is a cheap filler for manufacturers and has the huge side benefit that it helps addict consumers to their product.)

Natural Or Artificial Sweeteners?

Humans love sweets. It's in our genes...literally. Blood sugar (glucose) is our primary fuel, and a sweet taste on the tongue is a signal that blood sugar is about to rise. This deep love for sweet has led to some amazing advances in our ability to extract sugar from a wide variety of different sources.

It's fairly easy to see how humans learned to get the sweet nectar from sugar cane, maple trees and from honeybees, but we've also figured out how to get sugar from beets, corn, rice, agave, coconut and more. Eating any of these natural sources of sugar will cause the predictable rise in blood sugar that anyone would expect after eating something sweet. Modern agriculture has allowed massive amounts of these refined sugars into the food supply. In the quantities currently consumed, regardless of its source, it's a toxin and it promotes inflammation. Added sugars, even the naturally derived varieties, need to be limited.

Modern technology has also allowed us to eat high-tech sweet tasting chemicals that have virtually no effect on blood sugar. Saccharin (the pink one), aspartame (the blue one) and sucralose (the yellow one) are all examples of modern chemistry making its way into your food and drink. Although these chemical sweeteners don't directly raise blood sugar levels, they have been associated with increased rates of obesity, neurological problems (like migraines) and a host of other issues. These synthetic compounds are best avoided entirely.

The most recent addition to the rainbow of little sweet packets is the green one. Rebaudioside A or Reb-A is an extract made from the leaves of the Stevia (sweetleaf) plant. This product is surprisingly sweet, and like the synthetic chemicals above, has minimal impact on blood sugar levels. It is still a highly processed product, and probably not something you want to consume in large quantities.

During this program, as your sugar consumption decreases, you will notice that your taste buds will begin to become more sensitive to sweet flavors. After several weeks, most people continue to prefer their treats a bit less sweet. Small amounts of honey and maple syrup are the only sweeteners that you should eat.

Grains

"Oh beautiful, for spacious skies, for amber waves of grain..." Those flowing fields of wheat have become a nutritional battleground. It's hard to believe that the tiny seeds of these grass-like plants have caused so much controversy and confusion. There are a few simple facts that will help you understand how grains fit into a long-term health plan.

What Is The Difference Between A Whole Grain And A Refined Grain?

A whole grain is the entire seed of a grain plant, including all three parts of the seed:

1. Bran: The husk around the outside of the seed which contains fiber, B vitamins and antioxidants.

2. Germ: The tiny kernel inside the husk that will eventually sprout into a new plant. It contains vitamins, minerals, protein, and healthy fats.

3. Endosperm: The large starchy portion of the seed that will nourish the germ as it grows. It is largely composed of carbohydrates.

When a whole grain is refined, the bran and the germ are removed, leaving only the starchy endosperm. Whole grains are healthier because they contain all of the naturally occurring nutrients in the seed. Some common examples of grain plants are wheat, rice, barley, oats, buckwheat, and quinoa.

Is There A Difference Between Refined And Processed Grains?

Absolutely! Refining grain involves the techniques described above whereby the bran and the germ are removed. Processing grain is what happens at a mill, where grains might be cracked, split or ground into flour. Processing is done on both whole and refined grains.

When you're shopping for breads, crackers and other processed grain products, it can be really tricky to figure out if a product contains whole or refined grains. In the case of wheat, when the whole seed is ground into flour and that flour (and only that flour) is used to make bread, the packaging will say 100 percent whole wheat. If the packaging doesn't say 100 percent whole wheat, you can assume that refined flour has been added to the mix.

The Whole Grains Council has developed a "100% Whole Grain" stamp that can now be found on many foods to help make it easier to identify whole grain products. Learn more here: www.wholegrainscouncil.org

For many people, a short trial of three to four weeks of complete elimination of wheat and all processed grains can be very eye-opening. That's right, nothing made with flour at all... no bread, pasta, tortillas, crackers or baked goods for three to four weeks! This can be a great kick-start, because most people who eliminate wheat and grains will lose significant weight and feel better. After a complete elimination, you can bring back grains but you should only eat whole grains (like brown rice or quinoa) as well as products like bread, pasta and cereal made from 100 percent whole grains.

The reputation of this humble protein sure has taken a beating lately, and for good reason. Back in the 1960s, there was significant work done on developing a version of wheat that was much higher yield. This hybrid wheat plant is known as "dwarf wheat" and it is now the primary wheat variety that is used in the industrial world. (Some estimates suggest that dwarf wheat is as much as 99 percent of the wheat used in the market.) Unfortunately, over time, we have discovered that dwarf wheat is more difficult to digest than older, heirloom varieties. This may be due to differences in the concentration and structure of the gluten proteins in the grain.

Gluten is a family of proteins found in certain grains, with wheat, barley and rye being the three most common ones. It is what helps bread have a spongy, chewy texture. It can also make some people sick. In a condition called celiac disease, patients have an abnormal immune reaction to gluten that can cause a very serious illness. Total avoidance of dietary gluten is the only treatment for this condition. On top of this, it is estimated that six times as many people have a condition known as non-celiac gluten intolerance. Again, a gluten-free diet is the treatment for this condition.

Many people find that following a gluten-free diet delivers significant benefits to their health and vitality, especially in terms of reduced inflammation. The good news is that with the prevalence of these conditions, food product manufacturers, restaurants and bakeries catering to gluten-free diets are popping up everywhere. Scientists still haven't figured out all of the exact reasons why gluten can be such a trigger for inflammation, but one thing is becoming increasingly clear: many people feel better on a gluten-free diet.

There are many conditions and symptoms that respond well to a trial of a gluten-free diet. Usually, three weeks of wheat and gluten elimination will make it clear whether you have an intolerance, though there are more precise clinical tests that can be carried out.

In addition to the major macronutrient groups (fat, protein, carbohydrate) discussed above, there are also some really important micronutrient groups that are an important part of anti-inflammatory nutrition. We will explore these in detail in the next section.

Accessory Nutrients

In addition to the main three macronutrient groups (carbohydrate, protein and fat), the anti-inflammatory approach to eating also includes other accessory nutrients which can come from food or supplemental sources.

Fiber

Ideally, you should be eating 35 to 40 grams of fiber per day. The average American eats only about 15 grams daily. You can increase your fiber intake by including more vegetables (especially beans and greens) and fruit (raspberries top the list). Seeds are also an excellent dietary source. Try hemp, flax, or chia seeds in a smoothie or as a topping on your oatmeal, yogurt, or salad.

You can also consider adding a plant-based fiber supplement like flax seeds. Please note that it is important to grind flax seeds. Ideally, grind them at the time of using them to avoid rancidity issues, since flax is a great source of omega-3. The body is not able to easily digest the outer hull of the flax seed, so if you don't pre-grind them they will simply move right through you without getting the benefits of the contents of the seed.

Fish Oil

If you have trouble adding two to three servings of fish to your weekly meal plan, you should consider adding a high-quality fish oil supplement to boost your intake of dietary omega-3 oils. Typical doses of fish oil are about three to four grams per day.

Bioflavonoids

This is a family of plant nutrients that impart the rich color to many of our favorite flowers, fruits, and vegetables. Bioflavonoids have potent anti-inflammatory and antioxidant effects, as well as impressive effects on the health of blood vessels. It is easy to increase consumption of dietary bioflavonoids because they are found in large amounts in:

- **Berries:** Blueberries, raspberries, blackberries, strawberries, and any other darkly pigmented fruits. If it will stain your clothes, it is high in bioflavonoids.

- **Tea:** Green tea is the best, but black and white teas are also good sources.

- **Coffee:** Yes, you read that right. Coffee is in! Twelve ounces per day, max.

- **Chocolate:** Dark chocolate (above 65 percent) with low sugar content is okay in moderation.

- **Red wine:** If you don't drink, don't start. But, if you do drink, drink red wine. Enjoy one glass per day during Phase One, and two glasses per week during Phase Two.

Some people with certain musculoskeletal conditions will benefit from supplementation with specific bioflavonoid complex blends.

Vitamins And Minerals

There are many vitamins and minerals that play an active role in the biochemistry of inflammation. The most important ones being:

- Vitamin A

- B-Complex Vitamins

- Vitamin C

- Vitamin D

- Vitamin E

- Vitamin K

- Magnesium

If you're thinking that a list like that means that you need to run out to the nutrition center to stock up, I have good news for you. All of the above (with the exception of Vitamin D, which you get from sunshine) are plentiful in the foods that are included within the food lists in all three phases of this program.

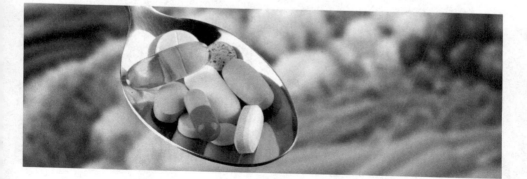

Herbal Medicines

Plant-based medicines can have powerful anti-inflammatory effects. There are hundreds of herbal medicines that can be used alone or in combination to support a healthy inflammatory response. Some of the most common and reliable herbal medicines for inflammation are listed below.

Turmeric
(Curcuma longa)

Also known as curcumin, this yellow Indian spice is much more than just an ingredient in curry. It is a very effective anti-inflammatory medication when used in the proper form and dosage. There are several proprietary formulations of curcumin that increase its absorption and potency.

Combining turmeric with black pepper, which contains "piperine," may enhance its effects.

Boswellia
(Boswellia serrata)

Known as Frankincense in the bible, the resin from the sap of the tree has anti-inflammatory activity comparable with synthetic pharmaceuticals. Similar to curcumin, there are a number of well-studied extracts available.

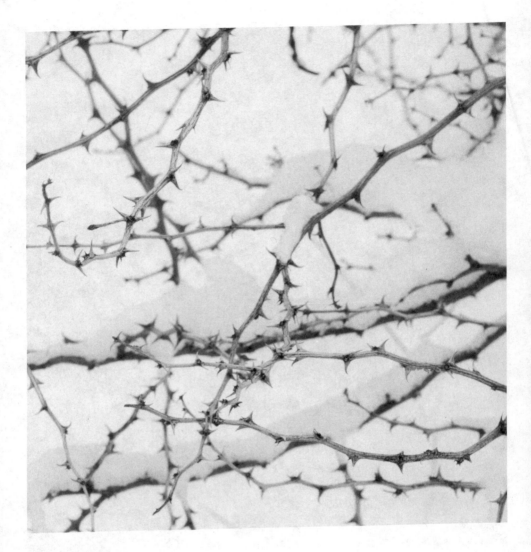

Devil's Claw
(Harpagophytum procumbens)

Despite it's rather evil sounding name, Devil's claw is an ally in the battle against inflammation. Extract made from the root has anti-inflammatory effects. Look for products that are standardized to contain reliable doses of "harpagoside" which is one of the active constituents in the roots.

Ginger
(Zingiber officinalis)

Ginger root contains a family of compounds called "gingerols" that have impressive anti-inflammatory effects. Add it to your food, drink it as a tea, and juice it with your other fruits and vegetables. You can also consider using it in a combination herbal anti-inflammatory supplement alongside some of the other herbal medicines listed here.

Hops
(Humulus lupulus)

Most famous as an ingredient in beer, hops cones also deserve some credit as an anti-inflammatory. Standardized hops extracts like Perluxan® can be really useful alone or in combination with other anti-inflammatory herbs.

There are many other botanical medicines that can be included in the diet or in supplements. Incorporate celery seed, cumin, rosemary, garlic, basil, holy basil, cloves, and cinnamon into your cooking or your dietary supplement protocol.

Living an Anti-Inflammatory Lifestyle

This program is centered on the diet as the primary told for reducing chronic inflammation. There is no question that food choices are a pivotal piece in this program, but there are some other important lifestyle considerations that we must not forget.

Anti-Inflammatory Living Requires:

Stress management: Research has shown that emotional stress can contribute directly to increased inflammation. The stress management strategies in this program can help your mind and your body.

- **Smoking cessation:** News flash: cigarettes are bad for you. They have no place in an anti-inflammatory lifestyle.

- **Personal hygiene:** Inflammation anywhere can contribute to inflammation everywhere. Pay special attention to your teeth and gums; tooth and gum disease has been clearly linked to systemic inflammation.

- **Limiting toxic exposures:** Learn about and minimize toxic exposures in your home, garden, workplace, and in your personal care products. Do what you can to eat clean and live green.

- **Moderate exercise:** When it comes to the intensity of exercise, be aware of "too much of a good thing." High-intensity physical activity can act as a stress and contribute to inflammation. Move your body for at least 30 minutes per day...and take it easy.

Now that you have a solid foundation of knowledge about how to reduce inflammation with your diet and lifestyle, you're ready to launch into The 21-Day Revival program full-steam ahead! I'll look forward to helping you through day-by-day for the next three weeks!

Take good care,

Dr. Josh

FIXING YOUR INFLAMMATION FOR GOOD

Welcome to The 21-Day Revival program guide. In this manual, you will find the three phases that make up the practical part of this program.

This plan is very detailed and prescriptive. It includes lists for each phase of foods to include and foods to avoid. The intention is to provide choices, but for some people, the recommended foods on the lists on the following pages may be ones that you are already aware that you need to avoid. For example, people who have celiac disease or those who are gluten-sensitive should continue to avoid eating gluten regardless of the advice in Phase One to replace white carbohydrates with 100 percent whole grain flour. Anyone with food allergies should, of course, avoid eating anything that they are allergic to, no matter what!

If you have any foods that you avoid for health reasons, continue to steer clear of those foods throughout the duration of this program. If there are healthy foods that you avoid because you're a picky eater, you "don't like vegetables," or have simply never tried them, that's another story. This is a perfect opportunity to step outside of your comfort zone and explore unfamiliar foods on the "foods to include" list for each phase of the program.

In addition to the changes that you'll be making to your diet, you will also be making some simple lifestyle modifications. You should be doing some gentle physical activity every day, along with some journaling each morning and evening. Each day, in written and video format, you'll also get lessons and tips about natural health and wellness that you can incorporate into your diet and lifestyle.

PHASE ONE

DAYS 1 TO 7

On Days 1 to 7, you will have three clean, nutritionally complete meals per day. Each major meal should be balanced. It will include a serving of protein and a serving of vegetables. You can substitute a smoothie for one meal per day, and one or two light snacks may also be included.

Your diet during this portion of the program will be built around minimally processed, single-ingredient whole foods. These nutrient-dense foods will be the fundamental building blocks of your diet during this period.

Here are some additional tips:

- Choose organic produce whenever possible.

- Aim for a rainbow of color when selecting vegetables and fruits.

- Fresh vegetables and fruits are ideal. Canned or frozen vegetables without added salt, sugar, or preservatives are allowed.

- Avoid refined white carbohydrates and replace them with whole grains and products like bread, pasta, and cereal made from 100 percent whole grain flour. Note: Avoid gluten if you already know you need to eat a gluten-free diet.

- Eat four ounces (1/2 cup) of protein in at least two meals each day.

- Eat animal protein sources like eggs, dairy, fish, poultry, and lean meat. However, you must only eat animal proteins that come from healthy, well-fed animals.

- Meat: This must be grass-fed or pasture-raised without unnecessary antibiotics or hormones.

- Dairy products (milk, cheese, or yogurt): These items must come from organic dairy farms unless you have a source of local dairy that you trust.

- Poultry and eggs: These must come from organically raised birds.

- Fish and seafood: These should include only wild-caught sources.

- You must completely avoid high fructose corn syrup, partially hydrogenated oils, artificial colors, artificial flavors, and preservatives.

FOODS TO INCLUDE

Vegetables	Fruit	Whole Grains	Protein	Fats/Oils	Drinks & Condiments
Organic whenever possible	Fresh or frozen, organic	May include breads, pastas, tortillas, cereals, crackers made from	With every meal		
• Arugula • Asparagus • Artichoke • Avocado • Beet • Broccoli • Brussels sprout • Cabbage • Carrot • Cauliflower • Celery • Chard • Collards • Corn • Cucumber • Eggplant • Endive • Greenbean • Jicama • Kale • Lettuce • Mushrooms o Okra • Onion • Peas • Peppers • Radish • Radicchio • Squash • Sweet potato • Tomato • Watercress	• Apple • Apricot • Banana • Berries • Blackberry • Blueberry • Cherry • Grape • Grapefruit • Kiwi • Lemon • Lime • Melon • Peach • Pear • Pineapple • Plum • Pomegranate • Raspberry • Strawberry	• Whole wheat • Oats • Brown rice • Quinoa • Buckwheat (Kasha) • Millet • Corn • Barley • Rye • Spelt	• Egg • Fish o Salmon (wild) o Sardine o Anchovy o Black Cod o Mahi-Mahi o Halibut (Alaska) o Herring • Beans/Legumes o All types • Poultry o Chicken o Turkey • Meat o Lamb o Beef (grass-fed) • Dairy o Milk o Cheese o Yogurt o Cottage Cheese • Soy o Tofu o Tempeh o Edamame • Nuts/Seeds (raw/unsalted) o Almond o Walnut o Cashew o Macadamia o Peanut o Pecan o Sunflower o Pumpkin o Hemp • Protein powder o Rice o Whey o Pea o Hemp	• Coconut • Flax • Olive • Sesame • Avocado • Grapeseed	**Beverages** • Clean water • Sparkling water • Herbal tea • Coffee (12oz max) • Fruit juice (dilute 50/50) • Vegetable juice • Rice milk • Nut milk • Coconut milk • Coconut water **Alcohol** • 1/Day max **Condiments** • Salt • Pepper • Herbs • Spices • Tamari • Vinegar **Sweeteners** • Maple syrup • Honey • Brown rice Syrup • Molasses • Stevia • Xylitol

The list of the foods that you can eat during Days 1 to 7 is extensive. As you can see, all of the individual items within each category are single-ingredient foods. They are foods that your great-grandmother would recognize. These are foods that you'll find on the outer perimeter of your local grocery store.

Most of the foods you will be consuming during these seven days will have no label at all. If they do have a label, the ingredient list will be very short. During this period, you will practice the skills that will allow you to build nutritious and delicious meals using these simple, delicious, whole foods as your building blocks.

FOODS TO AVOID

Carbohydrate			Protein	Fat	Beverages and More
Vegetables	**Grains**	**Fruit**			

• Limit white potato
• Avoid french fries
• Avoid potato chips
• Avoid canned vegetables with preservatives
	• Avoid foods made with "white" flour which includes virtually all commercially available bakery items	• Avoid dried fruits with added sulfur or preservatives	• Avoid factory-farmed:
			  o Beef
			  o Pork
			  o Poultry
			• Avoid non-organic:
			  o Dairy
			  o Eggs
			• Avoid all farm-raised fish and:
			  o Tuna
			  o Swordfish
			  o Shark
			  o Shellfish
			• Avoid smoked meats, fish and cheeses
				• Avoid harmful fats:
				  o Shortening
				  o Hydrogenated oils
				  o Partially hydrogenated oils
				  o Trans fats
				  o Margarine
				  o Cottonseed oil
					• Avoid:
					  o Alcohol
					  o Soda
					• Limit:
					  o Coffee (12oz max)
					  o Alcohol (1/day max)
					• Avoid:
					  o Sugar (refined and all processed variants)
					  o High fructose cornsyrup
					  o Saccharin
					  o Aspartame
					  o Sucralose
					  o Artificial color
					  o Artificial flavor
					  o Preservatives
					  o MSG
					  o Sulfites
					  o Nitrites

PHASE TWO

DAYS 8 TO 14

Now that you have completed Phase One, you have done the basic clean-up and you are ready to take it to the next level. You have decreased the sources of many of the most common triggers for inflammation, so your diet is cleaner and your body is nutritionally primed. You can now begin the process of making additional shifts that will ramp up your immunity and cool down inflammation.

During this period, you'll begin to add more anti-inflammatory superfoods as you wind down your consumption of animal protein significantly. You will cut down your sugar intake even further and you'll back down on the alcohol to just two drinks per week.

Phase Two is really important to get comfortable with because it is the portion of this program that most closely resembles the eating pattern that you should strive to continue when this program is over. It is not a vegetarian diet but it is power-packed with plant-based foods which are associated with decreased inflammation and reduced risk of chronic disease. This is the way that the longest-lived people in the world tend to eat, so it is clearly a long-term, sustainable solution.

As you did in Phase One, you will again:

- Choose organic produce whenever possible.

- Aim for a rainbow of color when selecting vegetables and fruits.

- Find fresh vegetables and fruits. Canned or frozen vegetables without added salt, sugar, or preservatives are allowed.

- Focus on getting at least four ounces (1/2 cup) of protein in at least two meals each day. Plant-based sources like nuts, seeds, and beans are highly encouraged.

- Completely avoid high fructose corn syrup, partially hydrogenated oils, artificial colors, artificial flavors, and preservatives.

Beyond those basic food rules, in Phase Two you will also:

- Eat only whole, unrefined grains. You should restrict refined grains and products made from flour, even if it is made from whole wheat. That means you should limit bread, pasta, cereal, and baked goods. Reminder: If you are celiac, non-celiac gluten sensitive, or know you need to avoid it, stay away from gluten!

- Liberally include beans into your meals and nuts/seeds into your snacks.

- Add herbs and spices to your food. Remember, spices are not necessarily spicy. Simply adding herbs and spices to your cooking can dramatically improve the anti-inflammatory effects of a meal.

- Limit your sugar intake and use only "whole food" sources like honey and maple syrup.

- Limit animal protein sources and focus on plant-based sources. You can eat one meat-based meal and two poultry-based meals during the seven days of Phase Two. You will only eat animal protein that comes from healthy, well-fed animals.

  ° Meat: This must be grass-fed or pasture-raised without unnecessary antibiotics or hormones.

  ° Dairy products (milk, cheese, or yogurt): These items must come from organic dairy farms unless you have a source of local dairy that you trust.

  ° Poultry and eggs: These must come from organically raised birds. Eggs that are fortified with omega-3 oils are encouraged.

  ° Fish and seafood: These should only include specific wild-caught swimming fish with fins and scales. No shellfish (like clams, mussels, oysters, or scallops) or crustaceans (like lobster, crab, or shrimp).

FOODS TO INCLUDE AND AVOID

Foods to Include	Foods to Avoid

✓ Carbohydrates:

- **Vegetables:** No restrictions! Fill half your plate with vegetables. Especially the colorful ones. Organic vegetables are preferred whenever possible.
- **Fruits:** Focus on the deeply pigmented ones, like berries and cherries. Fresh is best but frozen fruits are great too!
- **Whole grains:** Stick to grains that are in their whole, intact form. Brown or black rice, quinoa, buckwheat, and bulgur are great choices.
- **Beans:** Excellent source of complex carbohydrates and fiber as well as clean vegetarian protein. There are many varieties so mix it up with lentils, black, white, soy, pinto, kidney, and garbanzo.

✗ Carbohydrates:

- **High fructose corn syrup:** This stuff has no place in a healthy, anti-inflammatory diet. None.
- **Sugar:** Limit intake; sugar spikes insulin levels which contributes to inflammation.
- **Processed grains:** Restrict foods that are made from flour. When mills turn whole grain into flour, it makes the carbohydrates in the grain easier to break down which results in higher blood sugar spikes. White flour is worse than whole wheat flour but both should be limited.
- **White flour:** Breads, pastas, baked goods, snack foods, and pastries that are made with flour should be restricted.

✓ Proteins

- **Wild-caught fish:** High-quality protein and full of anti-inflammatory oils. Wild salmon, sardines, Arctic char, and black cod are great choices.
- **Omega-3 enriched eggs:** Clean protein and healthy fats.
- **Beans:** Beans made their way into both the carbohydrate section and the protein section. The lesson here is simple: eat more beans!
- **Organic dairy:** unsweetened plain yogurt and hard cheeses in small amounts.

✗ Proteins

- **Beef:** Factory-farmed cattle are fed almost entirely on corn, heavily medicated, and live in deplorable conditions. They are unhealthy animals and the meat from them is unhealthy for you.
- **Pork:** Hog farms are arguably worse than cattle farms. Stay away.
- **Poultry and eggs:** Again, factory-farmed chickens and turkeys are unhealthy animals that produce unhealthy meat and eggs.

✓ Fats

- **Olive oil:** Extra virgin olive oil should be the main oil you use in your kitchen.
- **Nuts and nut butters:** Walnuts, almonds, cashews, pecans, and nut butters without added ingredients are a part of an anti-inflammatory diet.
- **Seeds:** Hemp seeds, flax seeds, chia seeds can all be a delicious and nutritious addition.
- **Fish:** Cold-water fish like wild Alaskan salmon and sardines are nature's most reliable source of healthy, anti-inflammatory omega-3 oils.
- **Avocado:** There are high levels of monounsaturated fats in an avocado. Use avocado as a spread instead of mayonnaise.
- **Coconut:** Even though it contains saturated fats, this plant oil is healthy and useful for high heat cooking and baking.

✗ Fats

- **Trans fats:** Avoid them completely. If it says "hydrogenated" or "partially hydrogenated" do not eat it. Margarine and shortening are made of trans fats.
- **Butter, cheese, full-fat dairy:** Conventional dairy cows produce milk products that are loaded with pro-inflammatory saturated fats.
- **Beef, pork, and poultry:** Factory-farmed animals have unhealthy fats in their meat. You should restrict consumption of meat altogether, and only eat grass-fed, or pasture-raised animals.
- **Vegetable oils:** Although they may sound healthy, this is where the unhealthy Omega-6 fats come from. Stay away from soybean oil, vegetable oil, safflower oil, cottonseed oil, and palm kernel oil.

✓ Spices

These are the top ten anti-inflammatory herbs and spices, but there are many many more.

- Turmeric, ginger, cloves, cumin, paprika, sage, rosemary, cayenne, cinnamon, garlic. The more herbs and spices in your cooking, the better!

✗ Spices

Nothing to avoid here. Green light for *all* natural herbs and spices. Enjoy!

PHASE THREE

Phase Three is designed to be tough! It's a challenge that prepares you for the real world that lies ahead. It is not supposed to be the way you eat for the rest of your life. This phase is the end of your commitment to this program but it brings you right into the beginning of the rest of your life. The lessons that you learn during the most challenging part of this protocol are the ones that you will carry with you as you re-enter the real world with your new habits.

DAYS 15 TO 16

You will begin Phase Three with a liquid-only diet for 48 hours. You'll want to make friends with your blender...you're going to need it. A high-powered blender is ideal but a regular countertop model will be just fine. You can also make use of an immersion blender or a juicer if you have access to either.

The best way to succeed during these two days is to have three or four substantial "liquid meals" each day with sips of "liquid snacks" in between. This will prevent you from feeling hungry and keep your blood sugar stable throughout the day.

Typical liquid meals include:

- **Smoothies:** A smoothie that contains protein (nuts or nut butter, yogurt, protein powder) for breakfast as well as fruits and veggies is a great way to start the day off right.

- **Soups:** A blended, hearty vegetable soup will keep you feeling nourished well into the evening.

- **Homemade nut/seed milk:** A tall glass of a homemade nut/seed milk, especially one that includes the pulp, can be a meal unto itself.

- **Vegetable/fruit juices:** Blended fruit and vegetable juices can be a light evening meal.

Options for "liquid snacks" to be sipped throughout the day include:

- Clean water
- Lemon water (clean water with fresh lemon juice added, either served hot or cold)
- Herbal tea
- Fresh vegetable juices
- Vegetable broth
- Diluted fruit juices (dilute at least 50 percent with clean water)

Your daily caloric intake will be lower than usual in these two days, so do your best to keep your schedule as clear as possible and keep your activity level to a minimum. You can exercise moderately but keep it gentle. You should not schedule major events or social activities. During the fast, your focus should be on yourself and your goals for improved health and vitality.

When you have completed your 48-hour liquid diet, you will be entering the final phase of the program in a prime position to spend the next five days in a mode of optimized human nutrition. This is a time for pristine, maximal anti-inflammatory eating—no compromise.

DAYS 17 TO 21

On Day 17, you'll go back to having three complete meals per day. Your diet during this portion of the program will again be built around minimally processed whole foods but with a few important changes.

FOODS TO INCLUDE

As always, you will:

- Choose organic produce whenever possible.
- Aim for a rainbow of color when selecting vegetables and fruits.
- Find fresh vegetables and fruits. Canned or frozen vegetables without added salt, sugar, or preservatives are allowed.
- Focus on getting at least four ounces (1/2 cup) of protein at two meals per day.

You are free to eat the following animal protein sources:

- **Dairy:** Only plain yogurt from an organic dairy farm. Add your own fruit— no other sweetener!
- **Eggs:** These must come from organically raised birds.
- **Fish:** These should include only specific wild-caught swimming fish with fins and scales. No shellfish (like clams, mussels, oysters, or scallops) or crustaceans (like lobster, crab, or shrimp).

FOODS TO AVOID

For these five days, you will avoid the following items:

- **Wheat and gluten:** Even a few days of a gluten-free diet can make a huge difference in the way you feel.

- **Processed grains:** No breads, pasta, crackers, or baked goods. Whole grains like brown rice and quinoa are allowed.

- **Meat and poultry:** No red meat, no poultry, no pork. The only animal proteins you'll consume for this week are wild fish, eggs, and organic plain yogurt. If you want to try eating entirely vegan (no animal protein whatsoever) you are encouraged to do so.

- **Alcohol:** During Phase Three, no alcohol is allowed. (I like to tell my patients that it's easier if they pretend they are pregnant—even the men.)

- **Nightshades:** This plant family is a trigger for inflammation in some individuals. There is no way of knowing whether or not nightshades are a problem, unless you eliminate them for a period of time. Phase Three is the time. Nightshades that you must avoid are eggplant, tomato (including tomato-based sauces, ketchup, and salsas), white and yellow potato (sweet potato is okay), and peppers (bell pepper, chili peppers, etc.). Black pepper is allowed.

- **Corn:** This is a common trigger of inflammatory food reactions. Although non-GMO corn can be part of a healthy anti-inflammatory diet, you will be avoiding it during Phase Three.

- **Added sweeteners:** Your taste buds, your blood sugar, and your waistline will thank you.

- **Artificial colors, flavors, and preservatives:** Try to buy foods that don't have a label. Hint: look in the produce section. Limit packaged foods and you'll limit artificial ingredients entirely.

FOODS TO INCLUDE

Vegetables	Fruit	Whole Grains	Protein	Fats/Oils	Drinks & Condiments
Organic whenever possible	Fresh or frozen, organic		(With every meal)		

• Arugula
• Asparagus
• Artichokes
• Avocado
• Beets
• Broccoli
• Brussels sprout
• Cabbage
• Carrot
• Cauliflower
• Celery
• Chard
• Collards
• Cucumber
• Endive
• Green bean
• Jicama
• Kale
• Lettuce
• Mushroom
• Okra
• Onion
• Peas
• Radish
• Radicchio
• Squash
• Sweet potato
• Watercress
	• Apple
	• Apricot
	• Banana
	• Berries
	• Blackberry
	• Blueberry
	• Cherry
	• Grape
	• Grapefruit
	• Kiwi
	• Lemon
	• Lime
	• Melon
	• Peach
	• Pear
	• Pineapple
	• Plum
	• Pomegranate
	• Raspberry
	• Strawberry
		• Brown rice
		• Quinoa
		• Buckwheat (Kasha)
		• Millet
			• Eggs
			  (Only organic)
			
			• Fish
			  o Salmon (wild)
			  o Sardine
			  o Anchovy
			  o Black cod
			  o Mahi-Mahi
			  o Halibut (Alaska)
			  o Herring
			
			• Dairy
			  o Yogurt
			
			• Beans/legumes
			  o All types
			
			• Nuts/Seeds (Raw/unsalted)
			  o Almond
			  o Walnut
			  o Cashew
			  o Macadamia
			  o Peanut
			  o Pecan
			  o Sunflower
			  o Pumpkin
			  o Hemp
			
			• Protein powder
			  o Rice
			  o Pea
			  o Hemp
				• Olive
				• Sesame
				• Coconut
				• Flax
					• Beverages
					  o Clean water
					  o Sparkling water
					  o Herbal tea
					  o Fruit juice (dilute 50/50)
					  o Vegetable juice
					  o Rice milk
					  o Nut milks
					  o Coconut water
					
					• Alcohol
					  o None
					
					• Condiments
					  o Salt
					  o Pepper
					  o Herbs
					  o Spices
					  o Vinegar
					
					• Sweeteners
					  o None

Although the Phase Three food list does have some significant restrictions, it remains a very extensive list of foods that you can eat. This portion of the program was designed to help you to step out of your dietary comfort zone. Although this list is not exclusively vegan (fish, eggs, and yogurt are allowed) you will be avoiding meat and poultry, which is a big shift in the anti-inflammatory direction. You may even want to try a few days with no animal protein whatsoever!

You are encouraged to expand your palate and experiment with foods you've never tried before. This is the final phase of this program, so after Day 21, you will be re-entering the "real world" again. Use this time to listen to your body. You will learn some important lessons that you can take with you for the rest of your life.

FOODS TO AVOID

Carbohydrate			Protein	Fat	Beverages and More
Vegetables	**Grains**	**Fruit**			

• Avoid non-organic vegetables
 	
• Avoid nightshades:
  o Tomato
  o Potato
  o Eggplant
  o Peppers
 	
• Avoid french fries
 	
• Avoid potato chips
 	
• Avoid canned vegetables with preservatives
	• Avoid wheat entirely
	
	• Avoid all processed grain products made from flour including breads, pasta, baked goods, tortillas/wraps, crackers, cookies etc.
		• Avoid sulfured dried fruits	• Meat to avoid:
			  o Beef
			  o Pork
			  o Poultry
			  o Veal
			
			• Fish to avoid:
			  o Farm-raised fish
			  o Tuna
			  o Swordfish
			  o Shark
			  o Shellfish
			
			• Dairy to avoid:
			  o Milk
			  o Cheese
			  o Butter
			  o Cream
			
			• Avoid smoked meats, fish and cheeses
				• Avoid harmful fats:
				  o Shortening
				  o Cottonseed oil
				  o Hydrogenated oils
				  o Partially hydrogenated oils
				  o Trans fats/ margarine
					• Avoid:
					  o Alcohol
					  o Soda
					
					• Avoid all added sweeteners:
					  o Sugar
					  o High fructose corn syrup
					  o Saccharin
					  o Aspartame
					  o Sucralose
					
					• Avoid all:
					  o Artificial color
					  o Artificial flavor
					  o Preservatives
					  o MSG
					  o Sulfites
					  o Nitrites

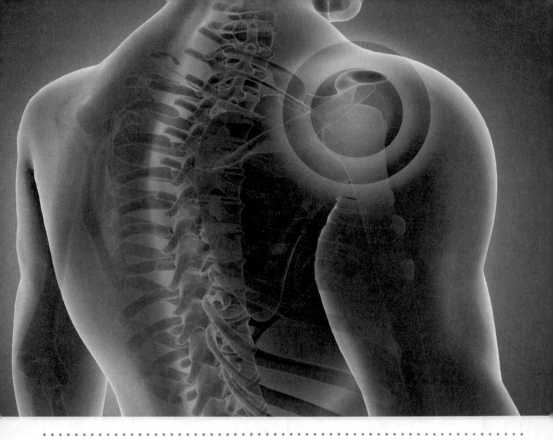

DAILY LESSONS

A short welcome note before you begin:

Whether you are sitting by a campfire, enjoying a candlelit dinner, or cooking on the grill, we can all agree that fire is a force of good. But when the fire leaps out of the fire pit, the candles get too close to the curtains, or the food stays on the grill too long, well, that's too much of a good thing. When it comes to fire, too much of a good thing can be dangerous, even devastating.

Just like fire, inflammation in your body can be a blessing or a curse. The inflammatory process is how your body naturally repairs and recovers from trauma, and that is most certainly a good thing. But when that essential repair and recovery function gets out of control, watch out! Uncontrolled, chronic inflammation is like a wildfire burning out of control. It is extremely dangerous and damaging, and it underlies virtually every chronic disease there is.

Do you remember Smokey Bear? He was a mascot designed to raise awareness about wildfires. Growing up in California, I'll never forget the image of him and his famous slogan "Only YOU can prevent wildfires." Smokey was right, prevention is the key—for both wildfires and inflammation.

The 21-Day Revival program is your personal handbook for the prevention and treatment of inflammation and all of the miserable symptoms it can cause.

This program puts the power in your hands. You'll get that fire contained and controlled by learning how to modify your diet, your lifestyle, and your behavior. And I'll be with you every step of the way. Check in daily and you'll find me right here for the next three weeks with daily lessons and inspiration to guide you as work your way through the program.

I know I'm looking forward to it...I hope you are too!

Day 1

Day 1 of this program feels both like an end and a beginning. Today marks the start of a new, healthier, anti-inflammatory way of living and eating. But of course, it also marks the end of your old way of living and eating...and I fully understand that it might feel a little nerve-wracking or intimidating. In fact, several people have told me that they feel like a runner on the starting blocks. On your mark, get set, you know what's next. Here we go!

At this point, you should be fairly familiar with the basic mechanics of the 21-Day Revival program (if you have not read through the *21-Day Revival Food & Nutrition Guide*, now would be a good time). The whole program is arranged into three main phases which each last seven days. Of course, today is the first day of Phase One...so you're off and running now!

Before we get too far down the track, it's important that we take care of a little bit of housekeeping. I know it's probably been quite a while since you've had a homework assignment but I have an important one for you today. Don't worry, this is not the sort of useless busy work you might remember from school—this one is extremely practical and useful.

HOMEWORK ASSIGNMENT #1

It's a two-part process: First, familiarize yourself with the foods on the "foods to include" and "foods to avoid" lists for Phase One (found on Pages 66 and 68). You might even want to have those pages accessible to you as you make your way into the kitchen...which is where this assignment gets real.

Second, fling open the doors of your pantry, then open up the fridge and the freezer. Get to the back of the shelves in there. Look for any foods that do not play nicely with the list of foods on your Phase One food list.

I'm not going to tell you what to do with the ice cream you found in the freezer or the box of cookies in the pantry. You can stash it out of sight, you can give it away, or you can trash it if you want. Let this be a time to reflect on what types of foods you've kept in there...and let it be a time to reconsider those choices.

The overall theme of Phase One is about doing the basic cleaning or "decluttering" of your diet. It's about eating a clean and simple diet that's based on familiar, single-ingredient foods. No matter how picky you are, there is a long list of things that you can eat this week. You will not starve!

One last thing: This week, a cup of coffee in the morning and a glass of wine in the evening is okay, but your first cup of coffee is your last cup of coffee and your first glass of wine is your last glass of wine. One cup per day! You'll survive, I promise.

That's plenty for today! Congratulations on getting off to a strong start. I look forward to checking in again tomorrow.

DAY 2

All great journeys begin with a single step...so congratulations on making it through Day 1! You've overcome that initial inertia, so now that you've started, you have overcome the biggest hurdle. Lots of people tell me that the hardest part was only having one cup of coffee or one glass of wine. And if that's true for you too, it might be something that you want to reflect on.

Today in Day 2, we are going to dig a little deeper into the distinction between processed and unprocessed foods. I'll start by saying that on this program (and in life after it), it is extremely important to read the ingredient list on foods that you are considering buying or eating. But there's an even easier way to make sure that the food you are eating is safe during Phase One, and that is if it does not have an ingredient label at all. Let me explain:

Carrots do not come out of the ground with a label that says how much fiber is in them. Avocados don't grow on a tree with a sticker that lists the fat content. Almonds are just almonds, bananas are just bananas. There are no other ingredients, no nutrition facts, no lists, no labels. Carrots, almonds, bananas, and avocados are single-ingredient whole foods, and they are my lunch for today. You might consider trying something similar this afternoon.

This does not mean that all of your food needs to be straight from the farm or the garden, but it does mean that you should be paying much closer attention to what you are actually eating. And that means that if you choose to eat something from a bag, box, can, or jar, you need to know what's in it. The most important part of the label is not the calories or the nutrition facts section—it's the ingredients section.

Usually, you'll find it below the nutrition facts box, sometimes off to the side and often underneath the folded section of the packaging. If you're looking at a box of oatmeal, the ingredients should be oats. That's it. If you're looking at a jar of peanut butter, it should be peanuts, and maybe salt.

If you see ingredients that you've never heard of or words that you can't pronounce, make a different choice. And if you see the words "high fructose corn syrup" or "partially hydrogenated oil," step away. Those are toxic food additives that have no place in an anti-inflammatory diet. Those ingredients, and the processed foods that contain them, are excluded throughout the entire duration of this program. You should keep them out of your diet for the long haul.

You're doing great so far! I'll be back with you tomorrow morning for Day 3. Take good care!

DAY 3

Welcome to Day 3! You're two days in, which (if my math is correct) leaves 19 more to go. I hope you're feeling good. After the first 48 hours, the benefits of a nutritious and balanced anti-inflammatory diet really start to kick in.

You'll also start to notice that as you incorporate more unprocessed foods, cooking is going to become a larger part of your life. When whole foods make up the majority of your diet, the preparation of that food becomes your responsibility rather than the job of a huge food processing facility. Learning how to prepare and cook new or different foods is a process—not an event. Be patient with yourself, and allow some time and space for experimentation.

Food preparation and cooking also requires some basic tools of the trade. The lesson for Day 3 is all about the most important tools that you'll need to make anti-inflammatory food preparation easy and fun. All of the following tools are things that every home cook should have on hand.

CHEF'S KNIFE

Although I have a whole set of different knives in my kitchen, the one I use the most by far is a Japanese chef's knife with an eight-inch blade. It's an all-purpose knife that can do all of the basic slicing and dicing you'll be doing throughout this program. The best knives have a blade that extends all the way through the handle, but as long as the blade is sharp, it'll work. It may sound counterintuitive, but sharp knives are much safer than dull ones because they do what you expect them to do.

CUTTING BOARD

A cutting board should be a prominent feature of your kitchen, not something that is stored away in the back of a cabinet. Our main cutting board is a beautiful handmade one that we got as a gift. It sits on our kitchen counter all the time, right next to the sink.

Cutting boards can be made of hardwoods, bamboo, silicone or even plastic. I like to use a large wooden board for most vegetables, and then a smaller one especially for spicy things like garlic or onions, which have a tendency to leave their flavors on the board even after a good rinse. It's also wise to have a separate, non-porous board for raw meats or fish to avoid contaminating your main vegetable board.

WOODEN SPOON

A good hardwood utility stirring spoon is a must-have item. Get a few in different sizes and shapes which you can use for just about any stirring or mixing you'll ever do.

CAST IRON PAN

A cast iron skillet should be getting heavy use in your kitchen for the next few weeks. A ten-inch skillet is a standard size and plenty big (and heavy) for most home cooks. The most critical thing to know about a cast iron pan is that it needs to be "seasoned" which refers to the baked-on coating of oil that makes the surface non-stick without the toxic chemicals used in conventional non-stick cookware.

A well-seasoned and well-maintained cast iron skillet will last a lifetime. It will work as well as any synthetic non-stick surface. It's important that when you wash your cast iron skillet, you only use water and a gentle sponge—no soap! Soap destroys the non-stick seasoning on the pan.

SHARP METAL SPATULA

Now that we're cooking on cast iron, it's a lot harder to flip the pan around because it's so darn heavy! So, to make the best use of a well-seasoned skillet, you'll need a sharp metal spatula that will help you get under the surface of whatever you've got cooking. My favorite one has a stainless steel blade and a sturdy plastic handle with all sorts of melt marks from times it has leaned against a hot pan. Rumor has it that a stainless steel paint scraper with a bent blade from the hardware store works just as well.

ALUMINUM BAKING TRAY

Some people call these cookie sheets or jelly roll pans, but you're not going to be using these trays for cookies or jelly rolls for the next few weeks. During (and after) this program, these trays are awesome for roasting vegetables. You'll need at least two of these in circulation and they are going to get lots of use. Look for trays that are 12 by 18 inches, or larger if you have an oven that can fit a bigger one.

SIX-QUART STOCK POT

This is what most people would call a medium-sized pot. On this program, you'll be using it to cook grains like oatmeal, rice, and quinoa, or anything else that gets cooked in liquid like lentils or other legumes. With the addition of a simple insert, this pot can also double as a vessel for steaming, which makes the six-quart stock pot a multi-purpose kitchen essential.

So those are the tools of the trade. I hope you get comfortable with them—you'll be using them a lot as we move along. I'll see you tomorrow for Day 4!

DAY 4

You've made it through three full days of anti-inflammatory eating... congratulations! Most people have noticed some changes in the way they feel at this point. Depending on what your diet was like before you started, you may notice some changes in your gastrointestinal function, shifts in your energy or mood, and some people will have even lost weight already. I hope you're feeling good!

The lesson that we are going to cover today is all about foods derived from animals. I like to think of these foods as the ones we get from:

- **Four-leggeds:** Generally, this refers to cows and pigs which give us beef, pork, and dairy products like milk, cheese, and yogurt.

- **Birds:** These are the winged ones, usually chickens and turkeys which give us poultry and eggs.

- **Swimmers:** These are the fish and shellfish that come from our oceans, lakes, and rivers.

Many people will feel a bit uncomfortable when they think about animal-derived foods in terms of the animals that they actually came from. But I think that if you do choose to eat animals, it's important to keep in mind what had to happen in order to get that meal onto your plate. And if those thoughts make you a little uneasy, good. Maybe you'll eat fewer of those foods, which would be a good thing for you, the animals, and the earth.

Excessive consumption of factory-farmed meat, poultry, dairy, and eggs is a major contributor to chronic inflammation and all of the serious chronic diseases that it causes. The Standard American Diet (SAD) has far too much animal protein and fat, especially considering that most of it is coming from unhealthy animals. Today, we'll learn a little bit about the four-leggeds and the birds and how they fit (and don't fit) into Phase One and the rest of The 21-Day Revival program.

Most of the meat, poultry, dairy, and eggs in the U.S. are produced in massive factory farms called "concentrated animal feeding operations" or CAFOs. These are high-tech industrial livestock operations that produce products with the same goals as any other factory: high efficiency, high volume, high profits.

In no way do these "farms" resemble the farms that most people think of with the big red barn and the windmill. Animals in CAFOs are confined in small spaces and fed unnatural diets (mostly corn) that maximize their production value. In most CAFOs, animals are given hormones and antibiotics which can then be found in the meat, dairy, and eggs they produce.

These industrial animal products are nothing like the small family farm version. Meat, poultry, eggs, and dairy that come from healthy (and happy) animals is healthier for you too. Cows that eat grass, clover, and other pasture plants produce meat and milk which has more "good fats" and less of the hormones and antibiotics found in conventional meat and dairy.

Chickens that get to move around, eat bugs, and consume a varied diet (like they naturally would) will produce better poultry and eggs. They are superior in taste and health benefits compared to the conventional alternative.

During Phase One of this program, you are free to eat meat, poultry, eggs, and dairy...but only if it came from a healthy animal. That means grass-fed, pasture-raised cows and free-range or organically fed chickens.

Eating animal products that come from healthier animals is a definite step in the right direction, but I'd also like you to think about decreasing the amount of animal-derived foods you're eating altogether.

People ask me all the time, "How much meat should I be eating?" Well, the best answer that I can give to that question is, "Less than you do now." And with that, I bid you farewell—I'll see you again tomorrow for Day 5. Onward and upward!

DAY 5

Welcome to Day 5! You're really moving right along now. I hope you are feeling well and learning something each day along the way. Yesterday we dug deep into the industrial food processing that is used in CAFOs to grow and process foods derived from cows and pigs (the four-leggeds), and chickens and turkeys (the birds). We learned about why these products are such a big problem.

Today, we're going to take a dive under the water to learn about the third source of animal protein: the swimmers. They get a whole day to themselves because there is so much to know about how to fit fish into this program and into a healthy anti-inflammatory diet in general.

When you revisit the guidelines for Phase One of this program, you'll see that fish and seafood are allowed and encouraged during this week...but there's a catch. (Pun intended.) If you are going to eat the swimmers, they need to be wild-caught.

In much the same way that CAFOs raise livestock as a commodity, large-scale fish farms do the same thing underwater. The fish and shellfish that are raised in most large-scale underwater farms live in overcrowded pens in contaminated water, eating a diet of fish chow that is made from all sorts of ingredients that a wild fish would never even encounter.

In fact, the diet of most farm-raised salmon is so bad that the farmers need to add a dye to their food supply to make sure that the salmon flesh has the right pink color to satisfy their hungry customers. When the diet of a fish is unhealthy and unnatural, the flesh from that fish is unhealthy and unnatural, too.

Many conventional fish and shellfish farms are also located in regions close to toxic water that finds its way into the pens where the fish are raised. The water in these pens is contaminated with chemicals including PCBs and other agricultural toxins found in runoff or wastewater. Not surprisingly, they're found in the fish too.

Compared to their farm-raised counterparts, wild fish generally have higher levels of healthy omega-3 oils and substantially lower levels of the chemical toxins found in farm-raised fish and shellfish. One notable exception is tuna, which is a very large and long-lived fish that can have high levels of mercury in its flesh, even though it is wild-caught. You should only eat tuna once per week or less.

So, fish and shellfish are on the menu...but only from wild-caught sources. And let's think outside the "fish stick" this week. I encourage you to get creative, step outside of your comfort zone, and maybe try a recipe for fish tacos using a grilled white fish like halibut or mahi-mahi. Or try making your own wild-caught salmon burgers using salmon from a can. You might also be surprised at how tasty a can of skinless, boneless sardines can be on top of a piece of whole grain toast with some lettuce and tomato.

DAY 6

Today is Day 6...almost the end of Phase One! Thanks for sticking with it, you should be proud of yourself. I hope that at this point in The 21-Day Revival program, you are getting more comfortable with the basic idea of eating whole foods that are minimally processed, and that you are getting more comfortable with eating plant-based meals.

As your diet begins to shift and lean more plant-based, it becomes increasingly important that you get to know your grains. And that's where we are going to focus our attention today. Simply stated, grains are seeds. We use the term grains to refer to the dry, hard seeds from a group of plants called cereals, which includes familiar crops like oats, corn, wheat, rice, barley, and rye.

Because of their shelf stability, versatility, and nutritional value, grains have played a major role in the human diet for millennia and have sustained and nourished generations of people from all over the world.

In their unprocessed form, any grain is simply a seed. And many of them can be cooked and eaten whole without any processing at all. A common example of a whole, unprocessed grain is brown rice which looks just like it did when it came off of the rice plant. But if you ever find yourself in a rice paddy, you won't see any white rice growing anywhere. Why? It's because white rice is actually brown rice with the outer husk removed—a step that happens in a processing plant, not in a rice paddy.

Every seed of every grain has a husk around the outside, which is known as the bran. When that outer covering is removed, it reveals the inner kernel of the grain which includes the germ and the endosperm. The germ is the part of the seed that will eventually sprout into a new plant, and the endosperm is the starchy part that is so commonly eaten or ground into flour.

During Phase One of The 21-Day Revival program, you've been eating only whole grains and products that are made from them. Avoiding refined grains and "white" carbohydrates is a big step in the anti-inflammatory direction because whole grains are extremely nutritious, packed with fiber, and will not cause the high blood sugar spikes that refined grain-based products are known for.

This is a great opportunity to try some new or different whole grains. Short-grain brown rice is one of my favorites, but there are many different colors and flavors of whole grain rice out there for you experiment with. And don't forget about oats, quinoa, and barley! They can all be part of your new and improved anti-inflammatory menu.

DAY 7

We have reached Day 7, the final day of Phase One. At this point, you're fully committed and getting this far bodes extremely well for you as we move through the next two weeks. Nice work! This business of diet and lifestyle change does not come easy so you should be very proud of yourself and your commitment so far.

Most of you who have followed the rules of The 21-Day Revival program will have already noticed some benefits so far. It's amazing how quickly the body responds to a change in the quality of the fuel. Better energy, improved mood, decreased pain, and significant weight loss are all common "side effects" of living and eating in an anti-inflammatory way.

Now that we are one-third of the way through the program, today is a perfect day to make sure that we stay on track with a quick review of the basic food rules and a deeper look at one of the most important ones.

The basic food rules that apply during all phases of The 21-Day Revival program are:

- Only eat during a 12-hour period each day.
- Eat meals and snacks slowly while sitting down.
- Your first and second meals of the day should include a portion of clean protein.
- Dinner should include a protein source, but this is not required.
- All meals must contain a vegetable.
- No seconds.
- Enjoy up to two healthy snacks per day if you are hungry.
- No food for at least two hours before bedtime.

I highlighted the rule at the top about only eating during 12 hours of each day because it's a rule that deserves some extra special attention. The idea we're discussing here is often called "intermittent fasting" and it can be a powerful tool in helping to extinguish the fire of chronic inflammation.

INTERMITTENT FASTING

In general, this is the practice of restricting your eating to specific hours of the day. As long as we do not eat in the middle of the night, most of us "fast" for at least six to eight hours each night already. In fact, that's why we call our morning meal "break-fast."

What you'll do in this program is just extend the time without food by a few hours. I designed this program to use a 12/12 schedule. For example, if you eat breakfast at 7 a.m., you should be done with dinner by 7 p.m., and not eat again until breakfast the next day. Not too hard, right?

If you are an overachiever, or if you are looking to more fully experience the benefits of intermittent fasting, I encourage you to push the schedule to a 16/8 plan. That means eight hours of eating and 16 hours of fasting, which would look more like eating from 9 a.m. to 5 p.m. and "fasting" in between. It's not as hard as it sounds—and the benefits are well worth it!

There is lots of new and impressive science on this method of eating. The findings are related to two main benefits. The first is that most people who eat this way will end up eating fewer total calories over a 24-hour period. Simply not eating between dinner and bedtime is an easy way to slice out hundreds of unnecessary calories every day, which leads to impressive weight loss without much effort at all.

The second reason why intermittent fasting is so useful for inflammation is a little more technical. It involves a cellular cleanup process called autophagy. This is an essential physiological process that is like an internal cleaning crew that removes cellular debris and "reboots" the system. The trick is that the cleaning crew does its best work when you haven't eaten for about 14 hours.

Many people eat so much and so often that they rarely get the full benefits of cellular autophagy...and this is one of the primary reasons for skyrocketing levels of inflammation and chronic disease.

I hope that intermittent fasting helps you and I look forward to seeing you tomorrow as we start Phase Two!

DAY 8

Welcome to Day 8 and the first day of Phase Two. You are a full weeks into this program now...two more to go! Great job so far. Phase One was all about cleaning house and getting familiar with the basics of a minimally processed, whole food, anti-inflammatory type of diet. I'm confident that at this point you are starting to feel some of the benefits of this approach in your body and in your mind.

At this stage in The 21-Day Revival program, many people have already noticed some improvement in energy, some modest weight loss, and a general sense of what it feels like to have lower levels of inflammation. Those are just a few of the benefits of an anti-inflammatory way of eating and they will continue to accumulate throughout the next two weeks and beyond.

Now, as we move into Phase Two, I want you to pay special attention to the eating pattern that you are following this week because this is the sort of dietary pattern that most closely resembles the way you should be eating once this program is over.

It's not a coincidence that this is also the way that the longest-lived people in the world eat, so it's clearly worth talking about. There is a lot of scientific evidence that says that the eating pattern of Phase Two is the way that humans ought to be eating all the time if they want to get and stay healthy.

The food rules for Phase Two are essentially the same:

- **Intermittent fasting:** Try doing 16/8 this week (for example, eating only between the hours of 9 a.m. and 5 p.m.).

- **No seconds:** Leftovers from today's dinner are tomorrow's lunch.

- **Organic whenever possible:** Better for you, the farmers, and the planet.

- **Aim for a rainbow of color:** Natural colors are beautiful, tasty, and healthy!

- **Limit processed foods:** Eat foods from real plants, not processing plants.

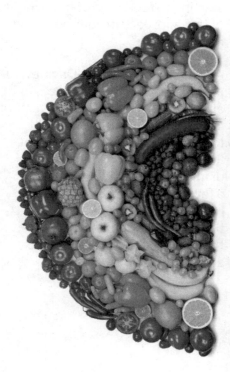

Those basic rules should be familiar at this point, but we are going to kick it up a notch this week. Here's how:

- **Only eat whole, unrefined grains.** That means we're not going to be eating anything that is made from flour, even if it's whole grain flour. You'll be limiting (or better yet, avoiding) bread, pasta, cereal, and baked goods. That's one big shift for this week.

- **Eat more plant-based protein.** We're still shooting for keeping a serving of protein in at least two meals per day but—and this is a big one—we're cutting back on the meat and the poultry. Instead, look for ways to add beans to your meals. Eat at least one bean-based meal as a substitute for meat.

- **Add spices.** Seriously, go out and buy a new jar (or better yet, a few new jars) of spices to add to your cabinet. Try turmeric, paprika, cumin, garlic, ginger and more! We'll talk more about how to use them later in the program.

DAY 9

You have arrived at Day 9! By this stage in the game, I have no doubt that you are making some changes that are making your life a little bit more difficult. You are eating less meat than you usually do. You are challenging your taste buds by including more vegetables. And you have even tried adding beans into your meals, as we discussed yesterday. All of those things are unfamiliar territory for many of you and that can make people a bit uncomfortable. Believe me, I understand.

So, as you near the halfway point on this journey toward an anti-inflammatory diet and lifestyle, it's important to take a step back. Look at some of the obstacles that you've encountered so far and give yourself a huge pat on the back! Then, it's time to get prepared for what lies ahead. The lesson for today is not about the food itself, but about your *relationship* with food—and how that relationship can improve.

To do just that, I'd like to share a story and a lesson that I have learned in my many years of advising patients about changing the way they eat. I saw a young man recently who came to me with a long list of medical problems, many of which would benefit from the dietary changes described here in this program. He was a young man who identified as a "meat and potatoes" person and it was very clear that he "does not like vegetables." It was almost like this was part of his identity...and I called him out on that.

My job in this situation was not to teach him how to cook vegetables, which was something he clearly was not going to do. My job was not to put him on a program that encouraged him to eat less meat and more vegetables. Instead, we spent some time working with his ideas of who he is, what stories he tells himself about food, and where those stories come from. And then we talked about how those stories have influenced his diet, his lifestyle, and his behavior—and most importantly, how those stories will end.

That is your lesson and your challenge for today. You have your own story about food. What is it? Where does it come from? How is it working for you? Are you ready to change it?

Perhaps you are Italian and pasta is something that you eat at every meal. Maybe you are a "meat and potatoes" person just like my patient was. Maybe you learned that a meal is not a meal unless there is bread. Maybe you've convinced yourself that you can't eat oatmeal without sugar, coffee without cream, or a burger without cheese. These are all just stories. Stories that others (like parents, grandparents, friends, and others) have told you, and stories that you continue to tell yourself.

You are in this program because you are concerned about inflammation. You are far enough into this program that you now understand that food choices have a major impact on the inflammatory process. So, if you are struggling with making the changes that need to be made, it's time to rewrite the story.

What I encourage you to do is to open up to the idea that stories can be changed. You can edit or revise your own story if it is not working well for you. The first step is to open up your mind to the possibility that there is such a thing as a different story...with a different ending. If you decide that you want to like broccoli, liking broccoli will get a whole lot easier. If you decide that you never eat past 8 p.m., the temptation of a midnight snack gradually goes away. When you change your identity from a soda-drinker to a water-drinker, avoiding soda no longer feels like a sacrifice.

Real, long-lasting change happens when we understand ourselves and the stories that motivate us. And if your story is pointing toward a disastrous ending, you can change it.

DAY 10

It's Day 10, and with that, we are officially halfway through The 21-Day Revival program! Yesterday, you spent some time thinking about your relationship to food. You got to reflect on the stories that inform that relationship, and if you don't like the way that story goes, you're allowed to edit it. You get to decide how it ends.

I've seen many powerful examples of how changing how we think and feel about food can have dramatic impacts on health. And that is especially true when people commit to eating better and eating less. But there is an unfortunate reality for many people, and it's one that we can't ignore: hunger.

At its core, hunger is a straightforward cue that tells us that it's time to eat. In fact, hunger is actually a lifesaving feeling when you consider what it meant for thousands of years of human evolutionary history. Throughout the majority of human history, our ancestors woke up every day wondering if they were going to get enough to eat. Death by starvation was a very real threat in daily life for our ancestors (and still is in some places), which meant that hunger was always a critically important message to heed.

In addition to hunger activating a behavioral response, it is also a powerful emotional trigger. Hunger is a warning. Hunger is a threat. Hunger sets off an emotional alarm, and our response is fear. Eating enough calories and maintaining stable blood sugar is vital for life, and that's why we are genetically programmed to fear hunger. We know that if we starve, we die... and hunger is the early warning signal. When food was scarce, those who paid the most attention to hunger were the ones who were the most likely to survive. We are all the offspring of those hungry *Homo sapiens*.

It's a pretty safe bet that nobody reading this will ever have to worry about starving to death because of drought, famine, or lack of access to food. Farming, agriculture, food processing, preservation, and transportation have come a long way in the last few hundred years. We have now reached a point where most of us have access to more food than we could ever consume in a lifetime. We should be grateful.

Yet, despite the blessing that most of us will never have to worry about starvation, hunger remains a powerful force in our lives. It still triggers fear and it still motivates food-seeking behavior just the way it did when food was scarce. For many people, hunger is so disruptive that they will go to great lengths to avoid it. Others get upset, irritable, grumpy, and short-tempered. The new term "hangry" (anger due to hunger) has become one of the internet's favorite words.

The lesson here is that the strong emotional reaction that we have to hunger is grossly out of sync with the reality of the modern-day food supply. We don't need to fear hunger anymore because we just ate a few hours ago, and we're going to eat again soon. Hunger is no longer a threat to our existence. You're not going to starve—trust me on this one.

In fact, people in the industrialized world today are far more likely to die of over-consumption than starvation. We are now overfed and overweight as a result. These days, hunger is actually more of a blessing than the curse it once was, and that's the frameshift that I have used to help many people get on the road to better health. If you are overweight, being hungry is okay. You're not in danger. If you're trying to lose weight and you feel hungry, that's your signal that you're headed in the right direction. Hunger is your friend.

Think about it like the soreness that you get from an intense workout. The soreness doesn't feel good, it's uncomfortable. But it's also a signal that your workout was effective. That unpleasant feeling is an indicator that you're on the right track. Think about hunger the same way. If you have weight loss goals and you're feeling hungry, you're on the right track.

I want you to reframe your mindset and reconsider your relationship with hunger. It doesn't have to control you. Shift your focus away from the hunger and direct your efforts toward eating a whole food, plant-based diet. I can assure you, not only will you survive, you'll thrive!

DAY 11

It's Day 11! You are over the hump and more than halfway through The 21-Day Revival program. I hope that you've found it useful so far. I know that many of you have found it challenging to eat outside of your comfort zone for the last ten days. FYI, that discomfort is an integral part of the program. And in case you were wondering, so is cheating.

There are many people who follow this program to a T. That's great, and it works best (like many things in life) when you follow the instructions. But after nearly 20 years in clinical practice, I have realized that not every person does exactly what I tell them to do. And that's okay. I learned this lesson from a patient that I saw while I was still a medical student, and it's a lesson that has stuck with me ever since. Here's the story:

The patient was a middle-aged man who was overweight, had high blood pressure, and type 2 diabetes. It was a pretty straightforward case. I felt like I had done a really good job explaining my approach, giving him advice on how to make the first steps to improve his diet and lifestyle, and made a few recommendations for herbal and nutritional supplements that could help him. I felt solid about how the appointment went and he did too. When he showed up for his follow-up appointment a few weeks later, I was confident that he was going to be doing well, and have better numbers to prove it.

I was wrong. He had not done one single thing that I recommended. No diet change. No physical activity. Never even bought the products I recommended. At first, I felt insulted. I questioned my own competence. I thought that I had done a good job, but clearly, if he did not follow even one shred of my advice, I was not as good as I thought I was. But here he was at a follow-up appointment and I wondered why he even showed up. If he didn't like what I had to say, why come back?

His answer? He loved my advice. He thought I did a great job too...and he told me so. The problem had nothing to do with me. He told me that our first appointment was awesome. He left feeling inspired and fired up to make a change. But when he got home after that appointment, real life was there waiting for him. And so was dinner. He quickly lapsed into old patterns, and before he knew it, it was time for his follow-up visit. He hadn't even found the time to pick up the supplements and he felt terrible about it.

The lesson here is simple: we all have real lives. We all have stresses and pressures that make life difficult. Sometimes that pressure makes it difficult to stay on track, especially when the track is something new, different, or difficult like this program is. Go easy on yourself. If you fall, get back up.

DAY 12

It's Day 12 and today I have a question for you. Is the table in your kitchen or dining room clear and set up for a meal? If your table has work, piles of paper, a computer, or anything else on it that is not directly related to eating a meal, then I have an assignment for you today.

HOMEWORK ASSIGNMENT #2

Clear that table! I want you to create a place where you can enjoy a relaxing meal. I encourage you to have some candles or a vase with fresh flowers on your table. Clear off everything else that is not related to serving or eating your meals.

You are well into Phase Two and we've talked a lot about what you're eating (and not eating) in The 21-Day Revival program so far. The lesson for today is different; it has nothing to do with what you're eating, but *how* you are eating it.

If you are anything like the guy I saw yesterday next to me in his car plowing through a sausage, egg, and cheese sandwich at a stoplight, you need to rethink not just what you're eating, but how you're going about the entire process. There are two main reasons why this matters:

1. When you are in a stressed ("fight or flight") state, your digestive process becomes much less efficient. When you are relaxed, your nervous system transitions into a "rest and digest" state which improves digestion, absorption, and gastrointestinal regularity.

2. Studies have shown that when people eat in a relaxed, social, and mindful way, they eat less and lose weight.

Mealtime should be a ritual. That does not mean that you need to have a fancy table or a candlelit dinner every night. It just means that when it's time to eat, you give your food the respect it deserves. Here are few tips for how to incorporate mindful eating into your meals today:

- **Slow down.** Consider setting a timer for 15 to 20 minutes and use that time to eat your meal.

- **Take small bites** and chew your food well. Savor the taste and texture of each forkful.

- **Put your fork down in between bites.** And even try using your non-dominant hand as you bring the food to your mouth.

- **Learn how to use chopsticks.** You'll quickly realize that it's a lot harder to shovel food into your mouth with chopsticks than it is with a huge spoon or fork.

- **Be mindful.** Take a moment before or during your meal to think about what you're eating, where it came from, what had to happen to get it to your plate, and how it nourishes you.

DAY 13

Today is your lucky day...it's Day 13! As we move toward the end of Phase Two, you have probably noticed (and even started to worry a bit about) how much less protein you've been eating. Our lesson for today is going to explain why that is—and why you do not need to worry.

The meat, poultry, dairy, and egg industries have many Americans convinced that animal protein is a critical ingredient in a healthy diet. This myth has been perpetuated by a great deal of media, most recently with all of the hype around the paleo diet. I'd like to set the record straight here: you do not need to consume animal protein to be healthy.

There are mountains of evidence showing that plant-based diets can provide more than enough nutrition (including protein) to our bodies and minds. While eating organic, grass-fed meats in moderation can be a part of a healthy diet, they absolutely should not be the center of all of our meals. When people ask me how much meat they should be eating, my answer is simple: "Less than you do now." The healthiest way to eat is to center your diet around plants.

There are two main reasons why you should be looking for ways to add vegetarian protein to your diet:

1. Plant-based protein sources are healthy foods. Simply stated, these foods are good for you.

2. Plant-based protein sources usually replace a meat-based meal. In other words, one more plant-based meal means one less meat-based meal.

BEANS AND LEGUMES

Beans and legumes are nutrient-dense foods that most Americans do not eat nearly enough of. There are so many varieties to choose from! Some of the most popular include black beans, butter beans, pinto beans, cannellini beans, lentils, chickpeas, and split peas. Along with plant-based protein, beans and legumes contain plenty of heart-healthy fiber, as well as iron, magnesium, potassium, zinc, and a wide range of other minerals. The science is entirely clear: beans are superfoods.

NUTS, SEEDS AND WHOLE GRAINS

Nuts and seeds are another category of nutrient-dense superfoods that you should be eating regularly. The nutrient profile of each different type of nut or seed will vary, but as a group, they reliably provide plant-based protein, fiber, vitamins, minerals, and omega-3 oils.

The pantry (and the fridge) in our house is always well-stocked with nuts and seeds. I just looked and took a quick inventory. I found the following: walnuts, pecans, cashews, almonds, pumpkin seeds, sunflower seeds, sesame seeds (white and black) chia seeds, hemp seeds, and flax seeds. They will all find their way into my morning oatmeal, on top of a salad, as a post-exercise snack, or as an ingredient in any meal on a daily basis.

Technically, grains are a seed as well. The difference is that most of what we call "grains" need to be cooked in order to make them palatable and digestible. Grains do contain amino acids and when they are prepared in their whole form (not refined or processed) they are also an excellent source of complex carbohydrates, fiber, vitamins, and minerals. Family favorites in our house include short grain brown rice, black rice, oats, quinoa, and buckwheat (kasha).

VEGGIES AND FRUITS

It may come as a surprise to many of you but fruits and vegetables contain protein, although not as much as the other vegan foods listed above. Combining fruits and vegetables with nuts, seeds, and legumes, however, is a great way to amp up the protein factor and the vitamin, mineral, and antioxidant content of your meals. Green vegetables, including broccoli and spinach, contain more amino acids than starchy vegetables—so load up!

Find ways to include plant-based protein into at least two meals per day and you're good to go!

DAY 14

Today is Day 14 which marks the end of Phase Two, and that means that tomorrow you'll be moving into the most challenging section of the program yet. I like to think of it as the steep section on a hike or the big hill on a bike ride—it's tough, but the view from the top makes it totally worth it.

One of the reasons why this program can be difficult for some people has to do with the restrictions on alcohol. At this point during the program, you have cut down on your alcohol consumption to two drinks per week. For some of you, that is no big deal. For others, it's the steepest part of the climb. Starting tomorrow, you are going to eliminate alcohol completely for the remainder of the program.

Before we talk about alcohol and inflammation, I want to let you in on a little secret from the doctor's office. At some point in our medical training, virtually all physicians learn that when we ask patients about their alcohol consumption during a medical history, the truth is probably close to double the amount of alcohol that somebody says they consume. Do people really lie to their doctors? Sadly, some people do, but it's also extremely common for people to underestimate and under-report the amount of alcohol that they consume in seven days. Many of my patients are genuinely surprised when they count the bottles and cans in the recycling bin at the end of a week.

You already know that consuming alcohol to excess is not good for your health. It is hard on the liver and can have pro-inflammatory effects if it's consumed to excess. This program is about improving your health by reducing your inflammation, and that's the main reason why I've set clear limits on alcohol consumption during the final phase. But there's another reason I set limits here as well... and that's about the value of the limits themselves. Allow me to explain:

Humans (and animals) feel safer and perform better when we know and respect our own limits. We say that "good fences make good neighbors" which is most certainly true in the neighborhood, but also with respect to your health. Having clear limits like "I don't smoke" makes it a lot easier to say no to a cigarette than someone who says, "I only smoke on special occasions" because they are now left to decide if today is a special enough occasion to justify a cigarette. If you simply don't eat or drink high fructose corn syrup, the temptation for it disappears. These sorts of limits are especially important when it comes to alcohol.

So, this next phase of The 21-Day Revival program will help you fortify those boundaries a bit. It will help you understand your relationship with alcohol and determine whether or not that relationship is a healthy one.

Many people think of alcohol as an essential part of their social experience. Others use it to take the edge off of stress and anxiety at the end of a day. For some people, it's just part of a familiar routine. And for many, it's a big problem.

This week, instead of a glass of wine, have a cup of tea. Instead of a beer, try making a spritzer with a splash of fruit juice and some unsweetened carbonated water. If a few drinks has always been part of your routine, I encourage you to change that routine this week and see how it goes.

One thing is for sure, it will make it a whole lot easier to get up the steep hill that's right around the corner. I'll see you tomorrow for Day 15!

DAY 15

Here we go! It's Day 15 and you are at the beginning of Phase Three, the final phase of your 21-Day Revival program. This first portion of the final phase is intense...and it was designed that way on purpose. I hope that you are prepared to slow your pace a little bit for the next 48 hours and really dial into the experience.

For the next two days, you'll be eliminating solid foods completely and relying entirely on liquids. Because you'll be consuming some calories, this is technically not a true "fast" so you don't need any medical supervision. You also don't need to worry about having any serious blood sugar regulation problems.

That said, you will probably feel hungry at times during the next two days... and that's okay. Remember (or even take a look back at) the lesson from Day 10 about how to redefine your relationship with hunger—you'll be fine.

There are several reasons why it can be useful to eliminate solid foods for a short period:

WEIGHT LOSS

Although this program is not a "weight loss program" per se, most people who want to reduce inflammation can also benefit from losing a few pounds, too.

GASTROINTESTINAL HEALING

The inner lining of the gastrointestinal tract plays a huge role in overall body health. New research has demonstrated that even minor superficial damage to the GI mucosa can adversely impact the immune system, which can increase inflammation. Give that hard-working and delicate lining a break every so often by eliminating solid foods for 48 hours! This can help improve the integrity of the lining and decrease the risk of chronic inflammation.

DETOXIFICATION

This is not about "purging" or "flushing" or any of the other buzzwords that are used to describe fad diets. Detoxification is an ongoing biochemical process that your cells are doing all the time. When you switch to a clean liquid diet, your digestive tract has less work to do and the cellular detoxification system gets a boost.

PSYCHOLOGICAL EFFECTS

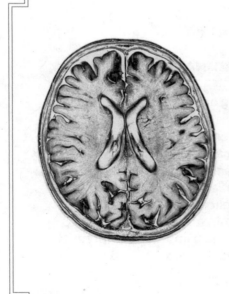

It's challenging to go without solid food for 48 hours. And when you face that challenge and succeed, you will come away from it stronger and with a profound sense of accomplishment. You'll also come away with a new and improved relationship with food and with your own ability to tolerate hunger. We'll dive into that conversation a bit deeper tomorrow.

LIQUID MEAL IDEAS

Some favorite liquid-only meals for today and tomorrow include:

- Smoothies (yogurt, nuts, nut butters, fruit)
- Blended soups or stews
- Milk alternatives (almond or hemp milks are easy to make at home)
- Vegetable juices
- Water (with lemon or lime)
- Vegetable broths
- Herbal teas

So, now is the time to pull that blender out of the cabinet and set it up on the counter—it's gonna get a workout for the next two days!

DAY 16

You have made it to Day 16, the second day of Phase Three and the second day of your liquid-only fast. You may be feeling a little altered or even a little woozy. Please take it easy today—this is the most intense part of the program. Your caloric intake is probably lower than it has been historically, so you are in a "calorie deficit" right now. For many people, this experience has physical, psychological, and even spiritual effects.

In fact, fasting has played a role in religious (and medical) history for thousands of years. Depending on the circumstances or the tradition, fasts can take many different forms. Christianity has several important fasting seasons, the most well-known of which is the 40 days of Lent which serves as an important time of self-reflection.

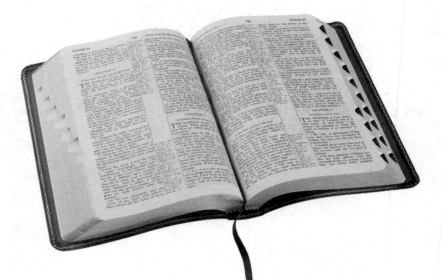

In Judaism, Yom Kippur is a famous (or infamous) "dry fast" with no food or liquids for a full 24 hours. Muslims celebrate Ramadan every year with a full month of fasting from sunrise to sunset. Buddhism and Hinduism also use fasting as part of their annual religious tradition. The fact that all major world religions use fasting for spiritual reasons is a testament to its physical, psychological, and spiritual impact.

I hope that you can think of today not as a day of deprivation but as a day of deeper self-reflection. I hope that you can use this fast to deepen your commitment to yourself and move your health forward in a positive way.

This is also a good time to put some extra energy into the daily program journal which is a part of this program. That is a great place to jot down your experiences, reflect on what you're grateful for, and measure your progress.

I'll see you tomorrow for "break-fast."

DAY 17

You are in the home stretch now... it's day 17! I hope that your 48-hour liquid-only fast was a positive experience for your body and mind. I know it was challenging, but I'm sure you would agree that it's the challenging things in life that lead to growth and change. Your metabolism is primed, your GI tract got a much-deserved break, and you are powering your way through the final phase of the program.

With just five days to go, today my goal is to help you understand the food rules for this final stretch. This portion of the program involves some experimentation...it's kind of like a test. You'll be doing a five-day "elimination" diet. The goal here is to eat an exquisitely clean diet that is free of the most common inflammatory trigger foods. Strictly avoiding these foods for a few days and then reintroducing them later can give you valuable insights into whether or not those foods are triggers for you.

Note: Please be aware that this is a much more strict diet than you'll be eating after this program is over.

For these five days, you will avoid:

- **Wheat and gluten:** Even a few days of a gluten-free diet can make a huge difference in the way you feel.

- **Processed grains:** No breads, pasta, crackers, or baked goods. Whole grains like brown rice and quinoa are allowed.

- **Meat and poultry:** No red meat, no poultry, no pork. The only animal proteins you'll consume for this week are wild fish, eggs, and organic plain yogurt. If you want to try eating entirely vegan (no animal protein whatsoever) you are encouraged to do so.

- **Alcohol:** This is a great time to reflect on your relationship to alcohol.

- **Corn:** This is a common trigger of inflammatory food reactions. Although non-GMO corn can be part of a healthy anti-inflammatory diet, you will be avoiding it during Phase Three.

- **Nightshades:** This plant family is a trigger for inflammation in some individuals. There is no way of knowing whether or not nightshades are a problem, unless you eliminate them for a period of time. Phase Three is the time. Nightshades that you must avoid include:
  - Eggplant
  - Tomato (including tomato-based sauces, ketchup, and salsas)
  - White and yellow potato (sweet potato is okay)
  - Peppers (bell pepper, chili peppers, etc.). Black pepper is approved.

- **Added sweeteners:** Your taste buds, your blood sugar, and your waistline will thank you.

- **Artificial colors, flavors, and preservatives:** Try to buy foods that don't have a label. Hint: look in the produce section. Limit packaged foods and you'll limit artificial ingredients entirely.

I know that sounds like a lot of things to avoid, but take a look at the Phase Three chart of foods to include and you'll see that there is plenty to enjoy this week.

Sometimes, an elimination diet like you're doing this week can have surprising results. If you're sensitive to something like wheat or corn that you eat every day, avoiding that food can improve your health in ways you never thought possible. As such, it's important to continue to keep track of how you are feeling in the journal each day during Phase Three.

Take good care, I'll see you tomorrow.

Vegetables	Fruit	Whole Grains	Protein	Fats/Oils	Drinks & Condiments
Organic whenever possible	Fresh or frozen, organic		(With every meal)		

• Arugula
• Asparagus
• Artichokes
• Avocado
• Beets
• Broccoli
• Brussels sprout
• Cabbage
• Carrot
• Cauliflower
• Celery
• Chard
• Collards
• Cucumber
• Endive
• Green bean
• Jicama
• Kale
• Lettuce
• Mushroom
• Okra
• Onion
• Peas
• Radish
• Radicchio
• Squash
• Sweet potato
• Watercress
	• Apple
	• Apricot
	• Banana
	• Berries
	• Blackberry
	• Blueberry
	• Cherry
	• Grape
	• Grapefruit
	• Kiwi
	• Lemon
	• Lime
	• Melon
	• Peach
	• Pear
	• Pineapple
	• Plum
	• Pomegranate
	• Raspberry
	• Strawberry
		• Brown rice
		• Quinoa
		• Buckwheat (Kasha)
		• Millet
			• Eggs (Only organic)
			• Fish
			  o Salmon (wild)
			  o Sardine
			  o Anchovy
			  o Black cod
			  o Mahi-Mahi
			  o Halibut (Alaska)
			  o Herring
			• Dairy
			  o Yogurt
			• Beans/legumes
			  o All types
			• Nuts/Seeds (Raw/unsalted)
			  o Almond
			  o Walnut
			  o Cashew
			  o Macadamia
			  o Peanut
			  o Pecan
			  o Sunflower
			  o Pumpkin
			  o Hemp
			• Protein powder
			  o Rice
			  o Pea
			  o Hemp
				• Olive
				• Sesame
				• Coconut
				• Flax
					• Beverages
					  o Clean water
					  o Sparkling water
					  o Herbal tea
					  o Fruit juice (dilute 50/50)
					  o Vegetable juice
					  o Rice milk
					  o Nut milks
					  o Coconut water
					• Alcohol
					  o None
					• Condiments
					  o Salt
					  o Pepper
					  o Herbs
					  o Spices
					  o Vinegar
					• Sweeteners
					  o None

PAGE 78

DAY 18

Welcome to day 18! Now that you are on a short-term elimination diet, it gets quite a bit harder to eat out, right? Well, I built the program that way on purpose...because I know that it is going to force you into the kitchen and a little bit outside of your comfort zone. I understand that this is challenging; you should be proud of the effort that you've put in up to this point! I'm confident that you are already feeling the hard-earned benefits that come from lower levels of inflammation and better health.

In seven simple words, author Michael Pollan summed up the main lesson for today. In his book *In Defense of Food*, he said, "Eat food. Not too much. Mostly plants." Let's explore each of those short sentences in a bit more depth:

1. **Eat food:** The idea here is to eat real, minimally processed food from the earth and avoid the edible "food-like substances" that your great-grandparents would not even recognize as food. Buy food that will eventually rot (many processed foods never go bad). Eat food that was made by people—not corporations.

2. **Not too much:** With rates of overweight and obese folks topping 70 percent these days, it is clear that people are eating too much and too often. Use intermittent fasting to your advantage. Let yourself be hungry. Stop eating when you are 80 percent full. No seconds. Tonight's leftovers are tomorrow's lunch.

3. **Mostly plants:** Most of your food should come from plants. One of the common dietary threads amongst the longest-lived people in the world is that they eat mostly plants. That does not mean that they are vegan or vegetarian, it just means that the majority of the food they eat comes from plant sources.

In the spirit of Michael Pollan's famous quote, I have a challenge for you. I want you to roast a vegetable each day for the next four days. Four days, four different vegetables, simply roasted with a little olive oil and sea salt. Broccoli, cauliflower, sweet potatoes, carrots, asparagus, or Brussels sprouts are all excellent options. The recipe could not be any simpler.

Once you have your vegetables of choice, slice them into bite-sized pieces (carrots and asparagus can be left whole) and arrange them in a single layer on a baking tray. Toss them with a little olive oil and sea salt, then bake at 400 degrees Fahrenheit. Check and stir every 15 minutes until veggies are brown and crispy on the outside and cooked through.

That's the challenge for the rest of the week. I look forward to seeing you again tomorrow for day 19.

DAY 19

It's hard to believe that it's already Day 19! I hope that you are feeling proud of yourself, and that you are experiencing the benefits of what an anti-inflammatory diet can do for you. Because the effects of inflammation can be widespread, decreasing inflammation can have far-ranging effects including improvement in energy, reduced brain fog, weight loss, clearer skin, better sleep, improved mood, less joint pain and stiffness, and just generally feeling better overall.

One of the most common "side effects" of reduced inflammation is that people want to take advantage of feeling better and start to move their bodies more. And that's exactly what we are going to focus on for today.

We have clearly established that, when it comes to inflammation, food really is medicine. And that idea can help you break free from the conventional perspective that medicine comes in a little orange bottle that you pick up at the pharmacy. There are lots of "medicines" that do not come in a bottle at all. And one of the most powerful prescriptions is this: movement.

Physical activity is one of the most potent medicines for the treatment and prevention of disease. In the same way that certain vitamins, minerals, and aminos are considered "essential" for life, so too is movement. Virtually all of the most common chronic diseases are fueled by inactivity, which is strongly associated with inflammation.

The large body of research on the dangers of sitting, and the excessive amount of time that Americans spend glued to their couches or chairs, led Dr. Anup Kanodia of Ohio State University to coin the phrase "sitting is the new smoking." It's an apt comparison. The solution to this is simple: we need to move more. Moving our bodies is one of the pillars of human health.

This might sound controversial, but there is one form of exercise that is the best—truly better than all the rest! The winner by a large margin is... walking. Every single day. A daily walk is the foundation of a movement-based lifestyle. Research is clear that walking for 30 minutes per day, in addition to other healthy practices, is a profoundly effective way to reduce inflammation and the disease risk that goes with it.

I walk or hike for 45 minutes each day, every day. I walk when it's hot and I walk when it's cold. I walk in the rain and, yes, I walk in the snow. I live by the famous saying, "There's no such thing as bad weather, only unsuitable clothing."

If you struggle to find the motivation to get out and walk, there is a simple "frameshift" that can make a huge difference in your attitude towards daily physical activity. When you leave the house for a walk, think that you *get* to go for a walk; this is very different than thinking that you *have* to go. Adopting the "get to go" mindset can change your relationship with exercise in a positive way. As you walk, enjoy the sights, smells, and sounds. Don't think of it as a chore.

To get yourself walking on a regular basis, I recommend committing to doing this every day. Not three times a week, not five times a week...every day. That way, you won't give yourself an excuse to put it off until tomorrow. Walking each day needs to be as routine as brushing your teeth—something that you never miss.

Have you gone on your daily walk yet today? If not, get out there!

DAY 20

It's Day 20 and I want to spice things up for you today...literally.

In the past, spices were a foundation of medicine and a cornerstone of global commerce. For most people today, they are just a collection of bottles collecting dust in our pantries.

As your dietary repertoire expands beyond this program, you should consider both the health and culinary benefits of spices. The flavor-enhancing qualities of these plant-derived seasonings are undeniable. Spices have been an integral part of Mediterranean, Asian, and Indian cuisine for thousands of years because they are a great way of adding zest to meals. The healing properties of spices have also long been recognized in these cultures as evidenced by their prominent place in Chinese and Ayurvedic medicines.

Sadly, the role spices can play in promoting health is comparatively (perhaps completely) overlooked in Western culture and in conventional medicine. The Standard American Diet (SAD) is extremely bland, largely because it contains very low levels of herbs and spices. And the people who eat the SAD diet have extremely poor health. This correlation has always made me wonder: could the deficiency of herbs and spices in the American diet be part of the puzzle when it comes to the epidemic of chronic disease and inflammation that so many people are suffering from?

One recent study published in the journal *BMJ* suggests that I might be onto something. It found that increased consumption of spicy foods was correlated with a substantial (14 percent) reduction in overall mortality.

Here are a few important things we are learning about some very popular spices and how they can bolster your health:

- **Cinnamon.** The evidence continues to mount that Ceylon cinnamon (also called "true" cinnamon) is an antioxidant powerhouse that can help regulate blood glucose and lower cholesterol. Not all cinnamon is created equal, so be sure to choose Ceylon cinnamon over the Cassia variety. The latter is lower cost but also lower quality.

- **Ginger** is loaded with a bioactive compound called gingerol, which is a natural oil with powerful antioxidant and anti-inflammatory properties. It is widely known for its anti-nausea effects but is also has antimicrobial, muscle relaxation, and positive digestive effects.

- **Garlic** is one of the most versatile herbs on the planet. It is rich in allicin, which helps lower cholesterol and blood pressure. Garlic is also a broad-spectrum antimicrobial agent.

- **Saffron** is widely used in Mediterranean countries (particularly Spain) where it is used to add flavor to dishes like paella. Animal studies show it is rich in a compound called crocetin, which is heart-healthy and has been proven to work like an antidepressant to improve mood and energy.

- **Turmeric** has been used in India for thousands of years to flavor cuisine and dye textiles, and used as an Ayurvedic medicinal remedy. It is loaded with bioactive compounds (especially curcumin) that counteract inflammation, improve circulation, and boost neurotrophic factors that promote cognitive health.

- **Cumin** is the second most popular spice worldwide (right after black pepper). It has been used for thousands of years as a digestive aid, to fight infections, and reduce coughs and respiratory problems.

- **Paprika**. According to a 2016 *Plant Foods for Human Nutrition* report, just one serving of paprika delivers one of the most potent doses of antioxidants you can get anywhere.

- **Oregano** has been used to add flavor to meals for thousands of years, but this Mediterranean herb is chock-full of phytonutrients, natural antiseptic agents, and antioxidants. The antibacterial properties of oregano are so powerful that researchers in the UK concluded that, "the essential oil from oregano kills MRSA at a dilution of 1:1,000."

- **Rosemary** is a Mediterranean herb from the mint family. Studies suggest it can improve memory, boost immune function, and help improve the hepatic detoxification system.

- **Cardamom**. A 2013 study published in the *Asian Pacific Journal of Cancer Prevention* found that cardamom was rich in anti-cancer compounds.

- **Cayenne pepper.** Derived from red peppers, this spice is used to amp up recipes across the globe. It's loaded with phytonutrients (including astaxanthin) which have anti-inflammatory, pain-relieving, and metabolism-boosting effects.

I hope that convinces you to dust off those little bottles in your spice rack and get cooking. I'll see you tomorrow for the final day of the program... Day 21!

DAY 21

You did it! Welcome to Day 21, the final day of the program. I hope it was an awesome experience. Speaking of all things awesome, it's not often that a medical research study gives me goosebumps...but this one did.

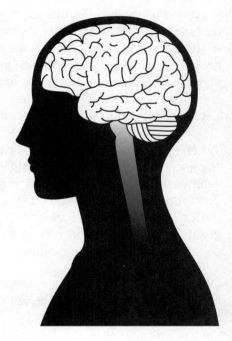

For those of you who understand that the mind and the body are connected, it should come as no surprise to you to learn that your physical health can be affected by your state of mind. Negative emotional states can have negative physical effects and positive emotions are associated with better physical health—including reduced inflammation.

There have been hundreds of studies that demonstrate this correlation. But in a recent study published in the journal *Emotion*, researchers from UC Berkeley took this idea one step further and asked a fascinating question: Out of seven common positive emotional states (amusement, awe, compassion, contentment, joy, love, and pride) researchers inquired about which emotional state had the most beneficial effect on markers of inflammation.

Here's how they set up the experiment. Participants in this study were surveyed using the "Dispositional Positive Emotions Scale" (DPES) which assesses how often and how intensely the seven positive emotions were featured in the daily life of the participants. They were then asked to provide a saliva sample. This was evaluated for levels of a compound called IL-6, which reflects levels of inflammatory activity. It turns out that the specific positive emotion that is the most strongly associated with decreased levels of inflammatory markers is...awe.

When I was a kid in Southern California, we used to say "totally awesome" to describe pretty much anything we thought was cool. I'm not sure we really ever knew what it meant, but in light of this research, I think we were onto something. When you start to look for opportunities to find awe, you'll notice that they are everywhere. A delicious meal. A gorgeous landscape. A great concert. A fun party. Time with people you love. Feeling good in your own body. All totally awesome.

With that, I wish you the very best. I hope that you find awe (and the lower levels of inflammation that go with it) in your life today and every day.

Take good care,

Dr. Josh